PORTS AND HARBOURS
OF THE NORTH WEST COAST

PORTS AND HARBOURS
OF THE NORTH WEST COAST

CATHERINE ROTHWELL

Catherine in Mullion Cove 1988: port trekking.
(Author's collection)

First published 2010

The History Press
The Mill, Brimscombe Port
Stroud, Gloucestershire, GL5 2QG
www.thehistorypress.co.uk

British Library Cataloguing in Publication Data.
A catalogue record for this book is available from the British Library.

ISBN 978 0 7524 5308 8

Typesetting and origination by The History Press
Printed in Great Britain
Manufacturing managed by Jellyfish Print Solutions Ltd.

CONTENTS

Introduction   7

Acknowledgements   8

Chapter 1   Early Shipping – The P&O Line   9

Chapter 2   Aldwater and Bourne End   11

Chapter 3   Ribchester – The Roman Connection   13

Chapter 4   Birkenhead and Liverpool   18

Chapter 5   Hackensall and Knott End   29

Chapter 6   Lytham, Freckleton and Warton   34

Chapter 7   The Lighthouse That Fell Down   45

Chapter 8   Blackpool – Piers and Satellites   47

Chapter 9   Torentum, Clevelas, Angersholme   56

Chapter 10   Manchester   59

Chapter 11   Preston   62

Chapter 12   Poulton-Le-Fylde, Wardleys and Skippool   65

Chapter 13   Fleetwood   77

Chapter 14   John Gibson – Master Shipbuilder   91

Chapter 15   'What Mean These Stones?'   95

Chapter 16	Glasson Dock	98
Chapter 17	Southport and Formby	102
Chapter 18	Lancaster	107
Chapter 19	Morecambe and Morecambe Bay	110
Chapter 20	I Am Sailing – The Manx Connection	116
Chapter 21	St Annes on Sea and Huntcliff	121
Chapter 22	Overton and Sunderland Point	124
Chapter 23	Arnside and Sandside	127
Chapter 24	Grange-over-Sands	130
Chapter 25	Milnthorpe and Greenodd	132
Chapter 26	Ulverston, Bardsea and Conishead	134
Chapter 27	Rampside and Piel Island	138
Chapter 28	Barrow-in-Furness	139
Chapter 29	Walney Island and Biggar Bank	143
Chapter 30	Millom and Ravenglass	145
Chapter 31	Whitehaven	149
Chapter 32	Workington and Maryport	153
Chapter 33	Silloth	156
Chapter 34	Haverigg and Seathwaite	159

INTRODUCTION

So much has been written and photographed on Westmorland, Cumberland and Lancashire shipping by knowledgeable men and experienced sailors, that when commissioned to prepare *Ports and Harbours of the North West Coast*, I quaked and questioned inwardly as to what more there was to say. Travelling that coast's length in the spring and summer of 1987 proved so fruitful of atmosphere, anecdotes, photographs old and new and above all, facts, that I was left with the usual difficulty: how to condense and what to omit, the latter always a painful process.

However skilfully presented, such a many-faceted subject must fall short of its larger-than-life origins. Ports, I discovered, died hard. It was not just ghost-faint letters on warm brick telling of past chandlers and net-makers, but dark-green glass floats suspended on fading ropes, ubiquitous sand and sea references in house names, pink and grey granite pebbles, gnarled moss stocks, lignum jetsam cropping up in gardens so close to the sea that, like the 'beach boys', they were spindrift-washed. An old boat served as a roof for one garden shed, surely the last of the Mohicans, and at what seemed like the world's end I found a mermaid figurehead; beautifully carved, paintwork washed pale to blue and gold, so faint the colour was almost gone. Sadly too – it was stuffed into a hedge of sea buckthorn. Why had no one wished to lovingly keep it?

Of course, there were the stories of old inhabitants: how the gangs of beach boys for example, scrubbed and salted cod on rock platforms; how each day the fish were spread in the sun and each night re-stacked into towers until cured ready for shipment. Many of the beach boys became sailors on ships in the Mersey.

Sitting quietly, as we often did, with a beef sandwich and flask of coffee, it was easy to conjure up those many scenes which, as one ex-sailor insisted, had been 'orderly chaos': foreign tongues amid the timbre of voices, clacking of capstan pawls as topsails went aloft; the softer scurrying sound of foresail rings soaring up the forestays; the grinding and groaning of bucket dredger mingling with steam whistles, screeching of gulls and frenzied last-minute loading of stores. The shipyard is permeated by scents of rosin, pitch, tar paint and new rope, shouts from the sail loft, the sound of long-handled axes and adzes wielded by men whose minds were the blueprints for the marvellous craft they put together, men who, when building waned at one port, would walk 50 miles to the next, carrying their tools. On to mighty Liverpool, where in 1862, 4,429 vessels cleared the port and 2,745 were registered; S. Price Edwards, Collector of Customs, could be justly proud of his port statistics.

More than a century ago, shipbuilding was considered cheaper in the north-west; thus Liverpool and Lancaster built for other ports, amongst them London, which also received sailcloth from Kirkham for the Navy. There was cheap labour and a plentiful supply of iron for anchors, chains and fastenings, wood for masts and linen for sails. Listed under dimensions and scantlings for Richard, built by John Brockbank on behalf of Edward Salisbury, are beams, stanchions, keel, planks, elm, fir, English oak, copper, brass and 'a Europa figurehead cut in London of proper dimensions for a ship of her tonnage.'

The hated Ship Money which helped to bring about a Civil War (even Clitheroe paid £5); the calls for England to be a Freeport (1641) ...'and universal warehouse to create trade and navigation'; the huge incidence of smuggling and its link with customs and excise; so many side-tracking, compelling ideas turned up in port trekking. Just think of this – Milnthorpe exported the famous Kendal Green cloth mentioned by William Shakespeare.

It was a privilege to join the trail, to follow in footsteps, to attempt, however inadequately, some sweeping aside of the cluttered detritus left by centuries and ports which exist now only in name, although 2010 visits show new business in some.

My great interest still lies in the ports and harbours that gently faded away like ghosts of old ladies retreating to care homes. But trekking in later years shows a resurgence in some, pleasure mixed with business. Like Gulliver struggling to rise, some have regained a footing. Others are well on the way.

Catherine Rothwell

ACKNOWLEDGEMENTS

The British Philatelic Bureau for parts of the first chapter, Lancashire Library, Blackpool Library, Ribchester Museum, Des Hanigan, Will Curwen, Michael Loomes, Ron Loomes, Barbara and Ron Strachan, The British Library, Kendal Library, the late Dr. Blacklidge, Richard Cavendish, Captain J. Ronan, the late N.T. Gazey, Meols Hall Muniments, Michael Goonan, Sheila Isherwood, Mr C. Humphreys, Lytham Heritage Group, Carleton News, Albright and Wilson, Kemsley Newspapers, *Lancashire Life*, Claire Sellick, Roger Hull (researcher at Liverpool Record Office), Liverpool Libraries, Liverpool City Council and Mersey Docks and Harbour Board.

CHAPTER 1

EARLY SHIPPING
– THE P&O LINE

The Peninsular and Oriental Steam Navigation Company, a grand name that can be reduced to P&O and still be known all over the world, is today a group of 200 companies operating in forty countries.

P&O 1837 Paddle Steamer. (Author's collection)

It started with but a few paddle steamers and a contract to carry mails, which they faithfully did for a hundred years. In 1822 a partnership was formed between Brodie Wilcox, a London Shipbroker and a Royal Navy man Arthur Anderson. In peacetime it was said they carried anything from machinery to giraffes. A Dublin ship owner joined them in 1835. He was Richard Bourne and two years later he signed the first Commercial Contract allowing him to carry mails by sea. The places covered included Falmouth (a deep-water port), Oporto, Lisbon, Vigo, Cadiz, and Gibraltar. Larger ships had to be put into service, big and strong enough to brave monsoon weather on the Calcutta–Suez line.

By 1845, having weathered a financial storm when the French succeeded in completing the Suez Canal, P&O steamers were plying to Singapore and Hong Kong.

Wrecks did occur and the mail was always saved first – even before the passengers. Ships carried civil servants, diplomats, ambassadors, missionaries and what became known as 'the fishing fleet of young ladies looking for husbands'. P&O carried emigrants and cargo after further expanding. All in all, a fleet for all seasons, and an undoubted success story.

CHAPTER 2

ALDWATER AND BOURNE END

―∞―

ALDWATH OR ALDWATER

In writing about small ports and harbours which have vanished entirely or of which only ghostly reminders are left, the many 'calling in' places along the coasts and rivers are also worth investigation as so much history surrounds them.

At Aldwater, where it is thought the Romans had a crossing on the River Wyre, there was first a ford then a ferry, a crossing probably there even before the Romans came. If the Roman port was where the River Wyre joined the River Lune (now submerged) there would surely be a ford or crossing place near there. Some 200 years later dispute arose between Sir Adam Banastre and the Prior of Lancaster about the right of way leading to Aldwater Ford. In 1330 an Agreement gave the right of passage on two routes through Sir Adam's land, one passage being to Aldwater, the other to the ford of Bulk (site unknown).

In 1276 Sir Adam and six of his retainers attacked the Prior, Ralph de Trune, taking him prisoner and holding him and his followers at Thornton.

Aldwater was used during the Civil War by both armies. Thomas Tyldesley's diary mentions 'a Scot with all his pack' being ferried over the river at Aldwater. Pedlars were known as 'Scotchmen'. By the 1860s the Shard Bridge Company built their Toll Bridge along Aldwath; all iron on pillars, costing about £13,000. The old toll board lists the types of vehicles that could cross, none of which you will see today, unless housed in a museum: a Curricle (a two-wheel chaise drawn by two horses), a Sociable (an open vehicle with seats at the sides), a Whiskey (a light carriage which one horse could pull quickly), and a Berlin (a four-wheeled carriage with a hooded seat).

At this point, rushes grew thickly towards the water's edge and rush gatherers made a living by gathering them, the rushes being used to make rush lights when dried and coated with wax, or they were used to strew on the floor of the church of St Chad in

Looking towards the newly built Shard Bridge, replacing the original built in 1864. The new bridge follows the line of Aldwath (Aldwater) Ford. (Author's collection)

Poulton. The entry of the Rush Cart was a half-yearly ritual. In 1786 travellers would call at the Bridge Inn, originally Ferry Boat House.

BOURNE END

Cornelius Bourne lived at Stalmine Hall in 1830 and had his own private 'calling place'. He wrote angrily to William and Matthew Lewtas, timber merchants (they built the barque *Hope* at Wardleys) about logs being floated down the River Wyre:

> I have to address you on the conduct of three of your men who were yesterday conducting a craft of two. I sent word to be as careful as possible when rafting timber past my weirs. The men aboard the raft yesterday from downright carelessness ran foul of the weir.

Cornelius' fear was that the salmon ladders situated at various points would be damaged. Stalmine certainly got its callers on pleasure or business-bound for it was known as 'the flower garden of the Fylde'. The Hall had heated channels within the high-wall of the gardens for the growing of peaches, grapes, nectarines and apricots, a system quite ahead of its day.

Chapter 3

Ribchester – The Roman Connection

RIBCHESTER

The eleventh-century Court Treasurer, Richard Fitznigel, wrote of the Domesday Book ordered to be prepared by William the Conqueror:

> This book is called by the English DOMESDAY not because it passes judgement on any doubtful points raised but because it is not permissible to alter its decisions, any more than those of the Last Judgement.

The Domesday Book was last consulted for legal precedent in 1982, 896 years after it was written by the scribe of William the Conqueror. Ribchester lies on the north bank of the River Ribble which flows into the Irish Sea and is mentioned in scant terms in the Domesday survey:

> Land of the King, Amoundemess, in Preston. Earl Tosti Taxable. These lands belong there – Ashton, Lea, (then follows a list of 59 towns including Ribchester). All these villages and three churches belong to Preston. 16 of them have few inhabitants but how many is not known. The rest are waste. Roger de Poitou had them.

Roger did not keep them because he rebelled against William the Conqueror who ordered the Domesday Book to be prepared. Forty-six of sixty-two settlements in Amoundemess were deserted and laid waste, for William brutally suppressed any rebellion in Yorkshire and in Lancashire. Ribchester lay on a major route to the west coast and would certainly have suffered in this way but there probably was an inlet creek or a harbour, with the river being so wide and handy for floating equipment. On the banks of the Ribble at Ribchester was found the famous helmet, now in the

William the Conqueror's scribe preparing the Domesday Book. (Courtesy of the British Library)

British Museum, but for 1,000 years nothing was found about Ribchester's history. The largest fort in Lancashire in Roman days was, to give it its full title, Bremetennacum Veteranorum, situated at a nodal point. Roads led to Chester, York and Carlisle. Some 500 cavalrymen were stationed there – the gravestone of a Roman Cavalry man has been discovered and also granaries at Ribchester. John Leland, employed by Henry VIII as historian, says of it: 'great stones and antique coins be found there.'

As at other outposts, the shell of a once big settlement would house soldiers, veterans who turned to farming and who would no doubt also make use of the River Ribble for fishing and transport.

PORTUS SETANTIORUM

This was the harbour of that war-like tribe the Brigantes or 'dwellers in the waters'. Only the scribe Ptolemy of the city of Alexandria has recorded the port at all but long ago it could have been important. Exact location is a mystery but the mouth of the River Wyre seems a likely area. At one time, evidence of Roman occupation was sparse but more and more finds are crediting them with a presence in the north-west.

Hoards of Roman coins were found at both Hackensall and Rossall, amber beads and trinkets on Pilling Moss. The wonderful bronze helmet and the gravestone of a cavalry soldier found at Ribchester also suggest that Portus Setantiorum was a useful harbour worn into the sea like many others.

Above left: Catherine in Calderdale en route for Roman Ribchester in May 2010. (Ron Loomes)

Above right: At Ribchester, this tombstone of an Astrurian Cavalryman can still be seen. There is record of a Roman Cavalry officer being drowned in the River Ribble when the river was in flood. Perhaps the most noteworthy is the gravestone of Flavinus, standard bearer of the troop of Candidus. He died at twenty-five years of age, having served for seven years. (Photo courtesy Patrick Ramsey)

Below: Looking towards Bleasdale Fells from River Brock path and field walk to Ribchester. (Ron Loomes)

Left: Engraving reads 'This stone taken out of ye Foundation of a Roman Temple at Ribchester, 1811.' (Photo courtesy Patrick Ramsey)

Below: 'Entrance to the River Wyre at low water', Portus Setantiorum – the early geographer places this submerged port at the mouth of the Wyre river. It is on Camden's map. (G. Herdman lithograph)

HADRIAN'S WALL IN NORTHUMBERLAND

My late husband Eddie and I, in our rigorous 'port trekking', were amazed at how Roman stations were so strategically linked; lakes, rivers and mountains did not deter, nor marshland. Communication between these stations was very good, using trained messengers and swift-marching soldiers, well-fed and well-equipped. Temples, statues, armour, coins and altars dug up, and inscriptions carved in stone, all declaim an alert presence in the north of England.

Ribchester, with the departure of the Romans (at a time when the northern 'barbarians' needed extra attention), fell into obscurity. The stones and mile castles on Hadrian's Wall were shamefully pilfered, but the ancient historian Camden stated, 'It is written upon a wall in Rome, Ribchester was as rich as any town in Christendom.' At the time of the Romans, it ranked as one of the first cities of Britain; Hadrian's Wall being the northern limit of their empire.

The 73-mile length of Hadrian's Wall with its sixteen forts marked the northern edge of the Roman world. The fort at Vindolanda, the busiest administered from Carlisle for thousands of troops, had granaries, bath houses, butchers' shops, and all manner of provisions. Today, it still remains an astonishing ancient monument. In March 2010 a 'line of light' from 500 points along the wall illuminated its length, each beacon operated from a gas cylinder. The Romans who left 1,600 years ago would surely have been impressed by such a celebration and the precise planning that went into its organisation.

Ancient steps of Ribchester churchyard with sundial, once part of the Market Cross. (Photo Patrick Ramsey)

CHAPTER 4

BIRKENHEAD AND LIVERPOOL

—◦◦◦—

The first reference I found to the spot where Birkenhead grew up was 'Woodside Ferry opposite Liverpool, worth forty shillings a year.' The monks of Birkenhead Priory took passengers across the River Mersey for a modest halfpenny and twopence for horsemen. Morton's Patent Slip was established at Birkenhead in November 1826 so some shipbuilding had been done, but the report on the Birkenhead Dock Bill was not discussed in the House of Commons until January 1844. Two years later, after the first sod was cut, the Birkenhead, Lancashire and Cheshire Junction Railway gave impetus and on 5 April 1847, Lord Morpeth opened Birkenhead (Morpeth) Dock.

The first emigrant ship to sail from the port was the *Stranger*, bound for Buenos Aires. An iron steam frigate of 1,400 tons, named after the town, was launched from the building yard of John Laird on 30 December 1845. 1851 was also important, as Birkenhead Ferry was leased for fourteen years by Messrs Willoughby and water was first let into the 'Great Float'; the *Bess Grant* from Honduras, laden with mahogany, being the first vessel to enter. Signs of prosperity increased with the years: a grandiose town hall and turret clock, park library, gas works, cheese and cattle fairs as more and more shipbuilding, expressed in wood, iron and steel took place.

By 1855 iron shipbuilding had so developed that Lloyd's Register of Shipping, which lays down standards, first published its rules for iron construction, to be followed twelve years later by those for steel. Early iron ships still used to sail so design did not alter radically until steamships arrived. By 1890 Britain was building four-fifths of the world's shipping and amongst centres was Birkenhead on the Mersey where shipwrights, skilled platers, rivetters, caulkers and drillers gathered. The new Industrial Revolution drastically reduced the original 170 acres of docks and 10 miles of quays. Three years after threat of closure the world-famed shipyard of Cammell Laird laid the keel of a new submarine, the *Unseen*, on 12 August 1987, 108 years after the *Lord Gough*. Two months later the Royal Navy frigate HMS *Cambelltown* was launched.

Liverpool waterfront, the famous skyline photographed from the ferry approaching the port. (Author's collection)

LIVERPOOL

In the 1600s Liverpool was a creek under Chester but it grew to become a great city sending ships to all parts within the Cattegat and Baltic, Sweden, White Sea, all parts of Europe, southward of Cape Finisterre, Newfoundland, Mediterranean, Greenland, Canaries, Madeira, Azores, West Indies, West Coast of Africa, Cape of Good Hope, the Adriatic, Black Sea – all these destinations and many more are listed in the 1836 Liverpool Docks broadsheet. Shipping lines included T and J Brocklebank with iron and steel ships *Alexandra, Baroda, Chimsura, Belfast, Majestic, Khyber, Bolam, Bactria, Sindra* and *Holkar* built between 1863 and 1885, the last five by Harland and Wolff.

There was David Bruce's Dundee Clipper Line, the fleet of the British Shipowners Company, the Irish 'Stars' of J. Corrin and Company Star of Erin, Denmark, Albion, Persia, Greece, Germany, Bengal. And the shipbuilders names Dobie, Brown Birrell, Napier, Shanks, Steele Cornell Elder, Laird, Barclay and so on.

When the holds of Liverpool ships were stacked with merchandise as varied as cotton, goods, coal, guns, knives and machinery, it was indeed one of the greatest ports in the world and it continues to fight on as 'the city of change and challenge.'

Economic changes ousting British shipbuilding and steel industries have also altered the old docks system at what is now Liverpool Freeport. In its heyday Liverpool with

37 miles of quays was the country's greatest port after London and if Birkenhead was included, as in the 1902 report, exports surpassed even those of London. A container dock terminal at Garston now handles most modern cargo ships including bulk carriers up to 75,000 tons. Otterspool, a rubbish dump, has been landscaped with a 3-mile-long promenade, whilst the Albert Edward Dock has become a money-spinning museum for the tourist industry.

The Mersey Docks and Harbour Board domed offices, as an example, mirror the days when Lancashire took one-fifth of the cotton crop of the southern states of America and one-half of the Egyptian crop, spinning, weaving and re-exporting three-quarters of this vast amount as finished products. Thousands of cotton shipments arrived; millions of bales were handled by the port, the first recorded shipment being on 26 June 1757 when twenty-eight bags of Jamaican cotton were imported.

The railway lines of the Mersey Docks and Harbour Board, taking passengers on Boat Expresses to the riverside terminus, opened in 1895 with a special train from Euston connecting with the White Star liner *Germanic* for New York. Liverpool's greatness was at its zenith when the city published five important daily newspapers. The Journal of Commerce minutely recorded the movement of ships of all lines.

The three-masted sailing ship *Endeavour*, in her trip around the world, called at Liverpool. Here she is at Charlestown in Cornwall. (Author's collection)

A famous building on the waterfront of the River Mersey – the Liver Building with the Liver Birds on top of the towers (centre), June 2010. (Author's collection)

In 1870 the Revd F. Kilvert, a famous diarist, described the scene:

The salt air was lovely, the Mersey was crowded with vessels of all sorts moving up and down the river, ships, barques, brigs, brigantines, schooners, colliers, tugs, steamboats, lighters, everything from the huge, emigrant liner steam-ship with 4 masts to the tiny sailing and rowing boat.

We came back to Liverpool, got luncheon and went to see the Docks. Nothing gives so vivid an idea of the vast commerce of the country as these docks – quays and immense warehouses piled with hides, cotton, tallow, corn, oil-cake, wood and wine, oranges and fruit, merchandise of all kinds from all corners of the world.

I admired the dray horses, huge creatures, 17 hands high, more like elephants than horses. Liverpool boasts the finest breed of Flemish draught horses in the world.

Liverpool once claimed to be the second city in the empire and certainly the world's biggest ships belonged to that port. Liverpool joined in the amazing achievement of linking the inland city Manchester with the sea by means of the Ship Canal. Now as 'the city of change and challenge' Liverpool can look back to the first dock built in the eighteenth century which made history in being a wet dock controlled by floodgates. This set a pattern worldwide. Then came George's Dock, Canning Dock, Prince's Dock, Queen's Dock and Coburg Dock. The most famous is Albert Dock designed by Jesse Hartley, who was appointed by the Docks Board. Albert Dock was unique in having warehouses adjacent so that bales of cotton could be unloaded immediately the ships arrived. It is still a dock to be proud of, delighting thousands with its history.

Today's round the world adventurers tend to finish their marathon here. Liverpool's dockland eventually grew to 7.5 miles of docks and warehouses.

In the 1880s the 3,920 tonne *Sarmatian*, built at Greenock in 1871 and the 2,306 tonne *Waldensian*, were ships of the Allan Line of Mail steamers under contract with the government of Canada. Other steamships in the fleet of twenty were *Circassian*, *Canadian*, *Prussian*, *Austrian*, *Caspian*, *Manitoban* and *Corinthian*, sailing from Liverpool to Quebec every Tuesday and Thursday with alternative sailings to Baltimore via Halifax (cabin fare 18 or 15 guineas). Unsurpassed for elegance and comfort, these steamers made rapid passages. Rock bottom cabin fare was a mere 13 guineas but that did not include wines and liquor. At the time, Allan Brothers and Company occupied Alexandra Buildings in James Street. The Liverpool, New York and Philadelphia Steamship Company is represented by *City of London*, belonging to the Inman Lines, sister ships, all cities, were named *Antwerp*, *Baltimore*, *Bristol*, *Brooklyn*, *Brussels*, *Chester*, *Durham* and so on. Each of these steamers had an experienced surgeon aboard, no charge being made for medicine and attendance. Even in the 1880s it was an old-established line whose steamers were amongst the largest and fastest afloat 'replete with every comfort; ladies' boudoirs, bathrooms, gentlemen's smoking rooms.' Even steerage passage allowed an unlimited supply of cooked provisions served by stewards. Passengers could be forwarded to San Francisco, Australia, New Zealand, India, China and Japan, using the Great Pacific Railway. William Inman's head offices were at Tower Buildings, Water Street. Liverpool was the first British port to have a floating crane of 200 tons lifting capacity. Built in Holland for Czarist Russia, it was never delivered because of the Revolution but bought by Mersey Docks and Harbour Board in 1920.

The dominating feature on the Mersey waterfront is the Royal Liver Building, opened on Coronation Day, 20 July 1911, seventeen storeys high with towers visible for miles. Its 'Waiting Train' turret clock, designed and constructed by Gent and Company, electrical engineers of Leicester, then held the record for being the largest electrically-driven clock in the world. The four dials are each 25ft across, minute hands 14ft in length. Most interesting are the Liver Birds perched on the towers carrying 'laver', a type of seaweed, in their beaks; creatures said to have lived in the 'Pool', So from the mists of time, the birds which first appeared on the coat of arms 700 years ago as the eagle of St John the evangelist, the city's patron, passed into the folklore of this great northern port.

No book on north-west ports would be complete without mention of the Isle of Man Steam Packet Company's personnel and its magnificent ships, its long history and until recently its continuous connection with ports Fleetwood, Heysham and Liverpool. Hero David or 'Dawsey' Kewley (1850-1904) in his career as boatman saved thirty-five

WHITE STAR

EX-ROYAL MAIL LINE OF

AUSTRALIAN PACKETS.

These Magnificent Clippers, which have been so long and successfully employed in the conveyance of Her Majesty's Mails between Liverpool and the Australian Colonies, are despatched from

LIVERPOOL to MELBOURNE,

On the 20th and 27th of every Month,

FORWARDING PASSENGERS, BY STEAM, AT THROUGH RATES, TO

GEELONG, SYDNEY, HOBART TOWN, LAUNCESTON,

AND ALL PARTS OF AUSTRALIA.

STEAM IS TAKEN TO CLEAR THE CHANNEL, IF NECESSARY.

RED JACKET, O'Halloran . .	4,500	SHALIMAR, I. R. Brown . . .	3,500
WHITE STAR, — Kerr . . .	5,000	ARABIAN, W. Balmano . . : .	2,500
GOLDEN ERA, H. A. Brown .	3,500	ANNIE WILSON, — Duckett .	3,500
MERMAID, Devey	3,200	TITAN, — Sears	5,000

The Ships of this Line are known to the World as the LARGEST and FASTEST afloat, and are fitted up regardless of expense, to suit the various means of every class of Emigrants. From the Saloon to the Steerage every article of dietary is put on board under the careful inspection of Her Majesty's Officers of Emigration, who likewise superintend the proper disposal of the necessary light and ventilation. The Saloons are elegant and roomy. The Second Cabins are fitted up with unusual care, and Passengers in this class have Stewards appointed to wait on them. The Intermediate and Steerage berths are exceedingly lofty, and the sexes are thoroughly separated. A properly qualified Surgeon is attached to each Ship.

RATES OF PASSAGE.

Saloon	£45 to £60
Second Cabin	£25 to £30
Intermediate, according to Rooms . .	£17 to £20
Steerage	£14

As Conveyances for Fine Goods, these Ships have long had a preference, having uniformly discharged their cargoes in first-rate order, and goods sent out by them can be Insured at the Lowest Rates of the day. For particulars of Freight or Passage, apply to the Owners,

H. T. WILSON & CHAMBERS,

21, WATER STREET, LIVERPOOL.

Agents in Melbourne . . . . H. T WILSON & Co., 41, King Street.

Details of White Star Line journeys from Liverpool to Melbourne. (Author's collection)

people from drowning. John Kewley, a relation, was chief mate of the first *Mona's Queen*. So many famous master mariners and engineers served the company that comparisons seem odious but Thomas Keig may be cited as a good example. He ran away to sea at the age of twelve to join a Whitehaven brig, *Village Girl*, bound for North America. After seal hunting off Labrador he sailed in many voyages, eventually joining I.O.M.S.P. Company in 1865 to serve for fifty years. He held the bridge of every ship in the company's fleet. When he became Commodore, the company's leading ship was *Empress Queen*. In 1915 he took *Ben My Chree III* to Liverpool to be reconditioned for war service. A well-known Lloyd's surveyor once stated that Captain Keig knew more about the practical details of a ship than any marine superintendent he had ever met.

LIVERPOOL, 30 MAY 2010

On our last trek to present-day Liverpool – city of change, challenge and culture – it was a windy, sunny day and I was accompanied by my voyager son.

Moored in Albert Dock, gently bumping the granite sides was a lone sailing ship, an old workhorse renamed *Nauticalia* given over to water sports. The lofty majesty of the Liver Birds seemed diminished by the incongruous juxtaposition of utilitarian buildings. Nonetheless, beautiful contrast lives on in the perfect symmetry, a feast to the eye, of the warehouse architecture that today lines Albert Dock.

Cunard and Dock offices – note the 'Liver Birds'. (Author's collection)

Landing stage Liverpool, 1930. (Author's collection)

Above left: Sailing, diving and water skiing on Albert Dock, from this the one-time sailing ship renamed *Nauticalia*, May 2010. (Author's collection)

Above right: Old warehouses, Albert Dock, Liverpool, June 2010. (Author's collection)

Above left: Behind Tate Liverpool is the commemorative Emigrants Statue. From here many Liverpool Emigrants ships sailed to the New World. (Author's collection)

Above right: Anchor from an old sailing ship outside Tate Liverpool and the Maritime Museum, June 2010. (Author's collection)

Above left: Dirigo, moored at a north-west port, late eighteenth century, was known as a 'Yankee Hell Ship', its captain having the reputation of Captain Bligh of the *Bounty*. She was a four-masted barque who flew the Stars & Stripes flag and had been involved in blockade running during the American Civil War. (Author's collection)

Above right: The four-masted ship *Liverpool* wrecked off Alderney, 25 February 1902 – the largest sailing ship – a four-master. (Author's collection)

Liverpool was the only city chosen by Tate Modern to host 'Picasso, Peace and Freedom' in Britain, until August 2010 when it would transfer to Denmark. The Exhibition was thronged with Japanese, Chinese, West African, European and the British of course. So there you have it – change and culture.

The wonderful Maritime Museum was also open. In the sunshine and buffeting wind off the Mersey, the crowds seemed happy, especially the questing children, yearning to climb, if not to swallow the huge anchor, that icon by the entrance!

Wistfully my son Paul said, 'And remember Mum, *Queen Mary II* can still visit and does. That's quite a sight.'

Above: Canning Dock, Liverpool, 1920s. (Author's collection)

Left: The Burgess certificate, 1791. (Liverpool Record Office, by kind permission of Liverpool Libraries)

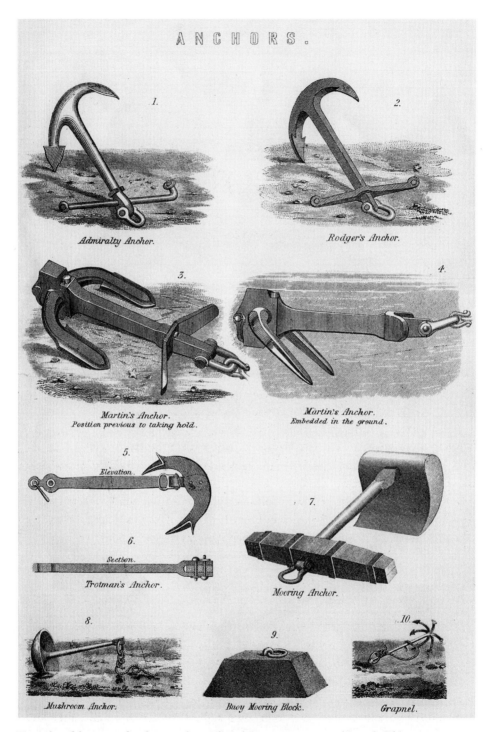

ANCHORS.

1.

Admiralty Anchor.

2.

Rodger's Anchor.

3.

Martin's Anchor.
Position previous to taking hold.

4.

Martin's Anchor.
Embedded in the ground.

5.
Elevation.

6.
Section.
Trotman's Anchor.

7.

Mooring Anchor.

8.
Mushroom Anchor.

9.
Buoy Mooring Block.

10.
Grapnel.

Examples of the types of anchors used on sailing ships – some were used in early lifeboat rescue.
(Author's collection)

CHAPTER 5

HACKENSALL
AND KNOTT END

⟞⟨∾⟩⟝

Hackensall Hall and the site upon which it was built are of ancient origin. Known as Hackensha by country folk of Preesall and Pilling, their antecedents knew it as Haakon's Hough and believed that the Norse invader Haakon used this as a calling place where he set up his first homestead.

The Great and Little Knotts which probably gave their name to Knott End, another calling place, bearing in mind an ancient ferry crossing, were removed when Captain Henry Mangles Denham ordered improvements in 1839 to be made for the navigation of the River Wyre. They were Scandinavian in origin.

A descendant, Geoffrey de Hackinstall, famed as a Bowman who served King John, was allowed to keep three casks of wine washed up at Knott End and for a while had right to Wreck of the Sea. Geoffrey allowed the canons of Cockermouth to set up a fishery in the River Wyre to augment supplies at Cockersand Abbey for on so many holy days the monks had to eat fish. The Hall in the photograph overleaf was built in the seventeenth century and has a stone dated 1685 which bears the initials of Ann and Richard Fleetwood. The Fleetwoods and Heskeths came here when Rossall Hall was flooded in 1833.

KNOTT END

In 1900, the official guide to Fleetwood was boasting 'Steamers every few minutes'. Cyclist Alan Clarke reported on the number of bicycles carried over in those glorious days when you could bowl along the Fylde lanes unhampered by traffic and unpolluted by petrol fumes. Books of twelve tickets for bicycles cost only 116d. The crossing of the River Wyre took ten minutes if your ferry boat did not get stuck on a sandbank.

The boats became characters in their own right. Children and adults alike loved them and came year after year for the ritual sail to Knott End. *Success* was sold for

Hackensall Hall. (Author's collection)

Remains of Cockersand Abbey Near Cockermouth and Glasson. 2010, the Chapter House. (Author's collection)

The remains of Cockersand Abbey, March 2010. (Author's collection)

£200 in 1887 and passed to Goole for further service. *Lune*, an ex-tug boat which was also used for pleasure trips up to Wardleys, home of the famous toffee, was bought for £105 in 1898. *Onward* followed *Lune* at a cost of £938, the first cabin cruiser capable of carrying 120 passengers. *Progress* (£1,312), built locally by Gibsons, boatbuilders, in conjunction with Robertson's, engineers, was a beauty made with solid oak frame and American Elm and pitch pine planking. She could carry 140 passengers. *Bourne May*, dating from 1901, had a deeper draught than any of the others. 'Who said the Ferry could not pay?' yodelled the triumphant *Fleetwood Chronicle* in an article on 20 July 1898. On 14 August 1905 a record 10,200 people crossed the river by ferry in one day.

Pilling (specially acquired for low water service) and *Wyresdale* joined the *Bourne May*. Fares were increased to 2*d*, cycles 3*d*, a time. A worker's ticket was then available for twelve journeys a week at the reduced rate of 116*d*. 500,590 were issued during 1932-3, obtaining a revenue of £5,569.

Some of the Croft Brothers, ferrymen over the River Wyre. Back: John Croft, William Croft, R. Rawlinson, Thomas Croft Junior. (Author's collection)

It had been well hoped that old favourite *Onward*, passed to the Navy, Army and Air Force Institutes to be stationed at Chatham in the Naval Canteen Service, could live again, the name being part of the Town's Coat of Arms, but as permission to call another ferry boat *Onward II* was refused, it was finally registered as *Wyresdale*, the largest steamer built in Fleetwood by James Robertson and sons. *Wyresdale*, a composite twin-screw steamer of 54 tons, did excellent service, but an explosion at 9.23a.m. on 12 April 1957 led to an official enquiry. The sudden development of a defect in the welded seam of the smoke tube, which split for a distance of fifteen inches, meant tragedy for engineers William Powell, William Thompson, John Wright and their shocked, grieving families: a sad end indeed for a craft which in its day had carried thousands of happy holidaymakers from all over Lancashire.

Left: Bourne Arms, Knott End; shipwrecked sailors found their way to this old inn, for example, from the *Utility*. (Author's collection)

Below: The *Bourne May*, ferry boat. (Author's Collection)

The ferry *Wyresdale* preparing to set off for Knott End, across the River Wyre. (Author's collection)

In those busy days, working with *Wyresdale* and *Caldervale* was *Lunevale*, ordered from Messrs. W.Y. Yarwood and Sons Ltd, Northwich, costing £6,085. She was a ferryboat of special form and construction, having a whaler-type stern, length 66ft 6ins, breadth 16ft and draught forward 3ft 3ins, aft 4ft 6ins. *Caldervale* did extra work, running up to Wardleys and out to Lune Deeps where ladies were hoisted up high in baskets to view Wyre Light poised on piles. For low-water services and spring tides *Caldervale* proved a boon. Built at Conway where she had been known as the *Queen Elizabeth*, this shallow-draught vessel, bought second-hand for £2,000, was a bargain and a favourite with the crowds.

As though foreseeing sad days and the end of an era, *Viking 66*, which came on the Ferry scene in the 1960s, was dogged with mechanical trouble from the start. Poor manoeuvrability frequently landed her on the sandbanks at Knott End on the fast ebbing tide. The butt of local ridicule, she resembled an ailing clown out of his time. Hiring relief boats is costly and past decades have been marked by shrill calls for the ferry shut-down. From a profitable undertaking it became a severe strain on the Borough's resources. In the busy days of the Second World War when refugees, civil servants and evacuees sheltered in the Fylde, 1.2 million passengers used the ferry service in 1942 alone. Now, one wonders nostalgically, with but a few passengers to deal with will the ferrymen come into their own once more, using oars and sailing boats to take people across the Wyre? More important, will Lancashire folks be willing to 'thrutch' as in the old days, 'thrutch' being real Lancashire for 'get out and push'?

CHAPTER 6

LYTHAM, FRECKLETON AND WARTON

—⟨∿∿⟩—

LYTHAM

Lytham's first outward sign as a port must have been 'Charlie's Mast' in evidence before 1840 almost opposite what was then the Clifton Hotel and consisting of lower, top and topgallant.

An aluminium mast now stands on the traditional spot on Lytham Hoe but Charlie Townsend's original utilised an old cart shaft. His lantern was the only guide for passing mariners and proved so useful a beacon when entering the treacherous River Ribble at night that the Lytham Improvement Commissioners maintained it after Charlie passed on. It appears in a photograph from 1895 by Hedges of Lytham when the town had become a popular watering place. On 29 July 1842, the Ribble Navigation Company's Report stated: 'The dock and wharf at Lytham are now satisfactorily completed and ready for the reception of vessels, during the storm of last week vessels were anchored there in perfect safety.' Cargoes bound for Preston had to be discharged at Lytham or Freckleton and carried onward by lighters.

Freckleton, which had rope walks and a large sailcloth mill, handled coal since 1720. Ships were built at Allanson's Yard on the River Dove near Pool Side. Freckleton dock also imported bricks and exported potatoes, grain and cotton goods from Kirkham. The Naze, where once stood the stillages, may well have been a landing point for the Romans.

At Lancaster assizes in the summer of 1824 Mr Clifton, Lord of the Manor, had established his claim for anchorage on vessels loading and unloading. Thomas Cookson was appointed Customs Officer at a salary of 10 guineas per annum, increased to 15 guineas ten years later. By 1850 when Lytham Customs House was built there were four officers watching for smugglers from the look-out tower. Contraband was stored in the cellars of this building which was also used as a mortuary for bodies washed up by the sea. A proposal to construct a ship canal from Preston to Lytham failed through lack of

Lytham Hall, 1931. Mr Harry de Vere Clifton sold extensive land around the hall for £1.3 million in 1971. (Author's collection)

Lytham Windmill and old Lifeboat House, January 2010. (Patrick Ramsey)

funds. Lytham stone lighthouse, built in 1848, fell down suddenly on 22 January 1863, undermined by the sea, a spectacular fall witnessed by George Gillett who was gathering mussels and William Cartmell, brother to Siah, keeper of Lytham's last lighthouse.

The town's hopes of becoming the much needed port of refuge on the north-west coast were dashed by Fleetwood's claims. With many contenders, for a number of years fierce arguments raged as to which site was best. Lytham urged that docks could be built on the River Ribble with a depth of water safe for vessels of 300–400 tons. Others favoured Wardleys Creek, ancient port on the River Wyre, but there was no great landowner to push that claim; Preston and Lancaster both had silting harbours. Wherever the port was built the railway must follow. Unfortunately for Lytham the death of the Lord of the Manor at this critical time may have shifted any balance in its favour. Rich, powerful Peter Hesketh with his idealistic plans for a combined town, port and watering place won the day. He promised in the 1830s a veritable 'New Liverpool' on that river referred to from time immemorial by experienced seamen as 'safe and easy as Wyre water.'

Sea captains of Lytham sailed round the world on ships from the windjammer days – *Queen of the Ocean*, *Hoghton Tower* of the White Star Line and *Dallam Tower*, the best-known ship. *Hoghton Tower* made a seventy-three-day voyage under Captain D. Murray on 26 June 1869 with seventy passengers. The first ship, a brigantine, *Grace*, was launched from Lytham shipyard in 1818. Around 1844, the Customs Watch House was built. After a furious storm on Christmas Day which destroyed the newly built wall along the sea-front, the schooner *Pheasant* from Preston, laden with coal was flung hard against the Watch House and one boat used by the Customs officers ended up near the railway. The fishing fleet (Lytham's was the first one along the Fylde Coast) was washed away with the pleasure craft.

Freckleton Pool, site of Allanson's Shipyard, April 2010. (Author's collection)

A goods warehouse on the north-west coast with coal trucks and steamer awaiting reloading and refuelling, 1910. (Author's collection)

Lytham Docks in 1950. (Author's collection)

The Watch House has now gone but in earlier times would be used, like that of Fleetwood, for keeping a wary eye on any ships. Lytham was established as a port before Preston and had four customs men employed also to apprehend smugglers.

Thomas Cookson met ships anchored in the River Ribble to collect Squire Clifton's dues.

Every Guy Fawkes night there was a great bonfire from driftwood and wreckage cast up on the beach. The lovely stretch of Lytham Green was originally prepared as a sea defence.

The Methodist Church of the 1860s with Corinthian pillars, one of Lytham's fine buildings. (Author's collection)

Above left: Market Hall *c.*1850, presented by Violet Clifton. (Author's collection)

Above right: Memorial to John Talbot Clifton in Sparrow Park, Lytham. Squire Clifton died in Algiers in April 1882. He was a great traveller, navigator and explorer. The Cliftons favoured Lytham as a north-west port. (Author's collection)

When the question of a port of refuge along the dangerous length of the western coast was fiercely discussed, Lytham was a high contender in the shape of Squire Clifton but Fleetwood won the day, a great persuader because of the high spending power offered by Peter Hesketh, later Sir Peter Hesketh Fleetwood.

An 1840 drawing of Lytham shows 'Charlie's Mast'. Erected by Charles Townsend, a mine of information on ships and shipping, it consisted of a cart shaft which proved such a useful landmark, the Improvement Commissioners agreed to its upkeep. It is still to be seen on Lytham Green. In the early days of Charlie, a lantern was placed on the mast and a wooden figurehead from a wrecked ship stood at its base.

A stretch off Lytham known as the Horsebank which had once been green pasture for cattle became good ground for a cockling industry, along with the famous potted shrimps from Lytham.

The Lytham Shipbuilding and Engineering Company was kept busy in its Dock Yard building craft needed on river ferry crossings. Boats went for use on rivers in Africa. The chain ferry for Windermere Lake came from the Dock Road yard and also the boat used in making the film in which Katherine Hepburn and Humphrey Bogart starred – *The African Queen*.

Cottages built for fishermen in 1800 have been well preserved in Upper Westby Street. Indeed much of this now bustling, modern town, whose first lifeboat was the Laura Janet, reflects the past. The Methodist Chapel built in 1868 with its imposing Corinthian pillars makes a grand statement. St Cuthbert's Church with the ancient cross in Church Road is commemorating St Cuthbert's coffin which is thought to have rested there, brought by the monks. Perhaps best of all eye-catchers is the white windmill and the 1805 Lifeboat House on Lytham Green. Sadly the Dock Yard has gone but Liggard Brook provides moorings for today's yachts. Lytham owes much to the Clifton family connected with Lytham Hall since the 1600s. Designed by the famous architect, John Carr of York in 1704 this beautiful, ancestral home was purchased in 1997 for the people of Lytham. Snowdrop walks in the wooded grounds of the Hall each spring are a delightful feature of Lytham's year.

FRECKLETON

Freckleton was one of the small, ancient ports dotted around the north-west coast which, in their day, were important. At Naze Point the Rivers Ribble and Dow meet to flow seaward beyond Warton and Lytham St Annes. The remains of the quay can still be found. Flat-bottomed boats brought coal daily from Wigan to Bunker Street at a spot known as Coal Hill. Grain, wood, slate and china clay were unloaded here and a shipyard established in the early 1800s. Schooners built here were *Ethel*, *Perseverence*, *Jane* and *Welcome*, Allanson Brothers eventually bought the yard. The demand for sailing smacks at Fleetwood was at one time so great that some were ordered from Freckleton. In 1972 a fire destroyed the

Eleanor Cecily lifeboat, Lytham. (Author's collection)

Liggard Brook and site of The Lytham Shipbuilding and Engineering Company Ltd . The yacht *Nancy*, belonging to the Clifton family, was moored in Nancy's Bay. (Author's collection)

boatyard. Rope walks and a large sail cloth mill were evidence of Freckleton's seafaring connections and 'Pool', but these are things of the past. Also in common with Poulton, the village lost one of the largest and oldest barns in the Fylde.

Investigations into Roman tracks between Naze Point, Dowbridge and Lund Church should bring some interesting history to light. Cromwellian forces are believed to have made crossings at the Naze at the time of the Civil War in the 1640s.

In the days when Elijah Rawstrone supplied the lamp oil and lamps for nineteenth-century Freckleton (he had a horse-drawn cart and stopped for custom on Heyhouses Lane at Fancy Lodge) there was a busy little port thriving at Freckleton. Today you have to look hard for signs of it.

In the eighteenth century Freckleton was a busy port with a boat-building trade in the yard of the River Dow north of Poolside farm. Several ropewalks (referred to by villagers as 'pads') were necessary. Along these pads, for which rent had to be paid, the ropes were plaited by means of a length of hem fixed to a post by several hooks. Keeping all lengths tight, the ropeworkers plaited. It took three men and strands depended on the thickness of rope required. When the plaiting reached the post, the rope was unhooked and passed to the chandlers.

Snowdrops in the grounds of Lytham Hall, January 2010. (Author's collection)

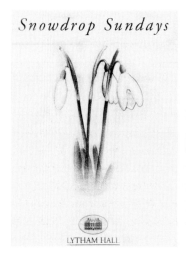

Above left: Snowdrop Sundays in the grounds of Lytham Hall have become an annual tradition. (Author's collection)

Above right: The Ship Inn, Freckleton, April 2010. (Author's collection)

Bunker Street, Freckleton. These houses were once the homes of handloom weavers and fishermen. (Author's collection)

One ropewalk ran parallel to Lytham Road which is shown on an 1845 O.S. map as Lamaleach Road. It ran from Goe Lane to behind Balderstone Cotton Mill. The other ropewalk on Green Lane emerged at 'the Tops' near the boatyard and by 1892 there were four ropewalks. At Kirkham Road and at Hillock Lane was a sailcloth and rope-making building.

When port trading was busy, sail making was also conducted in the cavernous cellars of the Ship Inn, a building also spoken of as lenient to smuggling. A lane from the Ship Inn lead to the Naze promontory and its sheltered pool, a natural feature formed by the Rivers Dow and Ribble. On the ebb tide this eighteenth-century port was waterless.

Captain William Latham, writing in 1799, stated that there was a Roman port at Freckleton Naze 'from the discovery of anchors and rigs of ships, even a whole vessel, it is evident that it was formerly used as a haven ... And the fort at the Ness or Naze was intended to keep a garrison for the security or defence of this part of the estuary.' Some modern historians corroborate this.

In 1842 the Clifton Estate constructed a dock with a wooden quay at Lodge Pool, Warton ('Nancy's Bay') into which the main sluice draining the mosslands discharged its water. Lytham Dock was used for thirty years (schooners unloaded opposite the windmill) providing safe anchorage for vessels awaiting the tide to Preston. A small graving dock, where boats could be built and repaired, was added.

The remains of a wooden 'stock' prove this to have been very old, possibly an eighteenth-century anchor – dredged up off the north-west coast of Lancashire. (Author's collection)

Items from the Lytham Hall Stewards' Accounts book, 1696-1704, refer on 19 January to 'Charges of a guide coming and going over the Ribble – one shilling'. From Guides House to the opposite bank of the river at Hesketh Bank is 3¼ miles.

The shipyard was near the Bush Inn, site of an ancient ford. Coal came in flat-bottomed boats from Wigan via the River Douglas which perhaps led to the naming of Bunker Street. Another sign of maritime connections was on the old vicarage which bore a lifebelt design. A new vicarage was built in Naze Lane. Freckleton is considered a port used by the Romans, landing at the Naze. It is thought that the twentieth Legion of the Romans linked with Ribchester in this place.

WARTON

Not far from Freckleton lies Warton with a once-important ford derived from guides who negotiated fords across the River Ribble from Warton to Longton Marsh and Banks Lane to River Bank. The Guides House Inn was of ancient origin, there being references to it in the Lytham Hall Steward's Accounts Book 1696-1704. A guide would see travellers safely from the rising ground where stood Guides House, to Hesketh Bank, 3 miles opposite where on a houseside was a stone plaque which read 'Jem Hornby, guide across the Ribble'.

In 1851 Henry Gomall was licensee at Guides House. A carved figurehead salvaged from a ship used to grace his dwelling. By 1918 the area had become a picnic spot where houseboats and deck chairs could be hired. It was possible to cross the ford on horseback when the tide was out but the guides' knowledge of channels was necessary.

'William of Warton', guide for forty years, had in his time lost ten horses. We know because in 1655 he applied at the Sessions for a grant towards the cost of a horse. Lower down from Guides House was the Manor House, one of the oldest farms in the Fylde, a sacrifice for Warton Aerodrome.

The Warton blacksmith's shop was on the village green. At Penketh Farm, now also gone, on the waterside near Guides House lived Granny Ellen Townsend, an indomitable country character born in the 1850s. She could remember the old Peg Mill, Beach Farm and the building used as a mortuary when drownings in the Ribble occurred.

A seafaring man lived at Mill House in the nineteenth century and a relic from the Peg Mill connects with Roman times in a hand mill or quem, bearing their traditional pattern of grooving, the best for grinding com. A beam, once part of a ship was built into a Warton cottage, perhaps another clue to the possibility that Warton, although it did not succeed as a small port, served as a landing place. Guides House Inn was demolished in 1945 when runways were needed for Warton Aerodrome.

CHAPTER 7

THE LIGHTHOUSE THAT FELL DOWN

⟞⟋⟍⟍⟞

January 1863 witnessed a great 'fall' in the Fylde, that of the massive, stone, elegantly designed Lytham Lighthouse which stood on the outer edge of the Double Stanner, 280 yards west of the Ribble Landmark. Situated almost opposite Lord Ashton's bungalow, this bank of stones was itself demolished by storms in the 1920s. St Annes was not in existence in February 1848 when first the light from its lantern shone across the water. Mariners navigating North Channel to and from the ports of Lytham and Preston found it very helpful, as they did the improvements to Wyre Harbour made under Captain H.M. Denham's instructions, further up the coast in Fleetwood.

On Thursday 22 January 1863, undermined by days of rough seas, the lighthouse fell exactly at a quarter past twelve noon. A boy of thirteen, George Gillett, of Cross Slack Farm, was gathering mussels not far away. Before his astonished eyes, the giant crumbled and scattered its bulk with a tremendous crash. Another witness was William Cartmell, nurseryman. His brother, 'Siah' Cartmell, was the last lighthouse keeper of the structure which was demolished in 1901 after serving for thirty-seven years, that particular one having been constructed of timber. Was it perhaps necessary to do a cut-price replacement? The original stone construction was built well inland on the sandhills and it is obvious that in 1848 they had no idea that the boisterous sea would eat so far into the land. It was one of many instances on the Fylde coast of the power of the sea's advance when backed by severe gales.

The timber-constructed lighthouse stood on a sandhill between Riley Avenue and Lightburne Avenue from 1864 to 1901 but after the new Cut Channel was made gas buoys were used and the Ribble Port Authorities cut down the lighthouse, fearing perhaps 'a bump in the night' if it was left.

A lighthouse is a picturesque landmark to lose. Research into the 1848 lighthouse evokes a detailed picture in the nostalgic mind's eye and warm admiration for the engineering skill of the Victorians. Erected under the guidance of Mr Tuach, architect of St Annes, at a cost of £1,400, its vital statistics were: diameter 14ft 6ins, height 52ft (with the lantern on top it was altogether 72ft high). Exclusive of the cool basement, where oil for the lanterns was stored, it stood six stories high. The ground floor was a workshop; the second floor had a projecting bay, semi-circular facing seaward within which the lower lantern was surrounded by a crimson glass funnel.

This produced a red light, heightened by a large, polished brass, concave reflector. The heated air was carried off by ventilating tubes based on 'Doctor Faraday's principle.' Above this was the floor occupied by the lighthouse keeper, a lookout commanding wide views of Lytham, Southport and Blackpool. The keeper did not live in; he had a house about half a mile away (one of the keepers was Mr Peter Walmsley, joiner and cabinet-maker). Above this was a small bedroom warmed by the funnel pipe of the stove from the room below and carried up to the very top of the building.

The attic storey contained the large lantern operated on the dioptric system and centrally placed, surrounded by a cylindrical lens and then a continuous window of plate so that the light was visible landwards as well as seawards. The Faraday tube ventilators could be regulated as required by weather or atmospheric conditions so that brilliance could always be maintained. The upper light, bright and constant, could be seen at 15 miles distance, the red light below at 9 miles distance, revolving and alternating quite distinct from others on the coast. What an interesting landmark to lose. When one recalls that the first attempt to erect a light to warn ships struggling with 'those infernal Ribble Banks' was Charlie's Mast, a primitive lantern lashed to a discarded mast from a wrecked fishing boat, Lytham's lighthouse of stone was progress indeed.

CHAPTER 8

BLACKPOOL – PIERS AND SATELLITES

━◦◦◦━

BLACKPOOL

Charles Allen Clarke, whose pen name was Teddy Ashton, was the editor of a local newspaper, *Northern Weekly*. He had a shop in Blackpool and produced a series of postcards in Lancashire dialect, very popular with workers from the mill towns who poured into Blackpool during Wakes weeks about 1910.

In 1916 he was writing for *The Blackpool Gazette* and *Liverpool Weekly Post*. His much-loved book Windmill Land tells how he visited the many windmills in the Fylde, meeting millers and country men and women. He was very interested in the beginnings of Blackpool… 'quaint old villages, historic places within a dozen miles of Blackpool'…'with cycle runs and motor coach routes'.

The photograph of Pennystone Rock to which Allen has waded at low tide shows his interest also in the village that supposedly was once on this site before being swallowed by the Irish Sea. The name derives from the penny pots of ale ordered from the inn or brewhouse, part of the village lost to high tides. Faintly in the background can be seen Norbreck Hall and the Rossall Hall gazebo. All parts of pastoral Windmill Land were his delight coupled with the wildness of the ocean and the wonderful sunsets. His awareness of the great height of the tower mills being useful visually to mariners as guides marking ships passages, inlets, estuaries, ports and havens: this crops up in his articles and classic book.

Blackpool's North Pier in 1913 was dubbed by many as 'the finest pier in Europe' and represents what might have been a port had it not proved phenomenally successful as a holiday resort. For the same reason it probably never developed a fishing fleet comparable to those of Lytham or Southport. Pool, meaning natural harbour or port, was a common term locally and Black Pool referred to the peaty area where Spen Dyke drained from Marton Moss into the sea. No other sizeable inlet occurred until the creek at the Gynn where occasionally ships could shelter, one such being a Scottish sloop saved by a lighted candle. Records bear out that it was a bad stretch of coast for shipping. At the time of this busy scene photographed by R.W. Lord of Poulton daily sailings were made by *Queen of the North*. In the Arcade played the Royal Roumanian Band, whilst *Greyhound*, *Wellington* and *Bickerstaffe*, other pleasure steamers, sailed from Central Pier: 'popular steamers, cheap fares, Douglas, Llandudno, Menai Bridge, Southport, Morecambe.'

Like 'Duke' Sutton's folly at Southport the first Uncle Tom's Cabin was made out of wreck timbers. With Harriet Beecher Stowe's story in mind, the figurehead from a wreck depicting a group of black sailors provided the inn sign. The Cabin was a vantage point for visitors watching ships bound for Fleetwood, Liverpool and Ireland, perhaps hoping for another spectacle like the two water spouts high as windmills. Many Liverpool ships came to grief on Blackpool shores, notably the *Crusader*, bound for Bombay with a cargo worth £69,000 and important government despatches.

The only fishing at present-day Blackpool is from small, privately owned boats and from the end of the piers. One early attempt to exploit the paddle steamer *Dhu Artach* as a primitive trawler, owned by Alderman Cocker, met with such opposition from Fleetwood fishermen that the scheme was dropped. From its fishing village origins to its success story as resort, Blackpool applied its talents to what it did best but it shares honourably in the splendid lifeboat record along this coast.

In 1930 the removal of graves from St John's churchyard, Blackpool, for the purpose of road-widening was a painful process for townspeople and parishioners who had ancestors buried in these graves. Also, because of so many drownings caused by storm and shipwreck, pity was expressed for unknown mariners lying in unmarked areas of the churchyard.

Big, sprawling, noisy Blackpool with its tradition of the 'Big One', candy floss and Kiss-me-Quick hats rose phoenix-like to overpower the landscape, seemingly Monarch or Ogre of all it surveyed. But Blackpool has its charming satellites in Bispham, Norbreck, 'Clevelas' and Thornton, the last two joined as Thornton-Cleveleys. They are ancient settlements in their own right and surprisingly managed to remain independent and be self-supporting for ages, perhaps because of their abiding link with land and sea.

PIERS

Along the coast of Lancashire especially, but also Cumbria, because of sandy stretches there arose many seaside resorts and what use were they without a pier?

Along with the craze for sea-bathing and the demands of the 'Wakes' crowds, piers became a 'must' and a pier with a jetty was ideal for pleasure boats to moor. The Blackpool steamer *Bickerstaffe* made sailings in the summer season. Very popular they were, apart from in 1923 when *Bickerstaffe* was hit by a freak wave which terrified the lady passengers. Blackpool, never a port, was good on piers.

Photographs of the crowds make one wonder how the planking could bear the strain of so many bodies. Blackpool, however in the late 1800s advertised in French to draw even more visitors. There was a College Français on the site of Queen's Hydro, South Shore.

In May 1863, North Pier opened, then came Central Pier in 1868 but, still not content with peerless pierage, a third pier followed. On the North Pier, the most popular pier of all with a jetty much used by fishermen, although heavy seas smashed it time after time, time marched on and helicopters flew out to the gas-rig from the heli-pad built at the end of a new jetty, which could also accommodate pleasure steamers unloading trippers.

Above: North Promenade Pier, Blackpool. (Author's collection)

Left: Blackpool Victoria Pier. (Author's collection)

Pennystone Rock, now split by tides. The site of old Singleton, inundated around the time of the Spanish Armada. (Allen Clarke)

Great Marton Windmill, demolished about the turn of the century 1899–1900, a landmark for ships at sea. (Author's collection)

BISPHAM

The ancient cross in the churchyard of All Hallows, Bispham could once have been a wayside or boundary cross. Brought into the churchyard, such crosses were often made into sundials. Sooner or later someone could not resist taking the dial and its gnomon (pointer) and this cross, like the Poulton one, has suffered likewise.

Two little village girls outside Moor Farm, Bispham. (Author's collection)

Anchorsholme, anciently known as Angersholme, shown when retirement homes were being built to meet the popular demand of city dwellers. (Author's collection)

Left: Bispham Village, 1890. The tea rooms are on the right, while Ivy Cottage on the left across street dates from 1600. (Author's collection)

Below: Bispham Village, the police station is on the left. This was the 1940s. (Author's collection)

Norbreck Road going up to the sea – Bandula on the left. Small shrimpers and fishing boats worked from here, Norbreck near Blackpool, in the 1890s. (Author's collection)

Left: Laying a sewage pipe in the summer of 1981, the dredger *Holland* came to grief in an unexpected storm. Dredgers were owned or hired by silting harbours for use along the north-west coast. (Author's collection)

Above left: Entrance to Jubilee Pier, Fleetwood, 1904. Lancashire and Yorkshire Railway Companies. (Author's collection)

Above right: Washed from the 'Red Banks' by sea, made into a sun dial at Norbreck: an erratic Ice Age boulder. (Author's collection)

Left: St John's churchyard, Blackpool, 1905. Amongst the graves were those of drowned sailors. (Michael Loomes)

Fanny Hall on cliffs opposite the miner's home, Blackpool. The building was demolished in the early 1900s. (Michael Loomes)

Rustic Cottage, 1900, Bispham Old Village. The archway is made of seadrift – some used whale bone which had washed up. (Author's collection)

Pearl, wrecked at Norbreck in October 1895. (Author's collection)

On this stone are the initials R.B. – Robert Brodbelt, a seventeenth-century parish clerk and a local character, was known to rest upon the steps of the cross.

The dial was made by John Hebblethwaite, dated 1704, its motto 'Die dies traditor' 'day treads on the heel of day'. John Hull actually presented the cross and his initials also adorn the cross. The Brodbelts owned land on the Banks of Bispham and some were seafaring men.

The well-known Lancashire dialect poet and writer Edwin Waugh stayed at Bispham and Norbreck. In 1860, staying at Norbreck, he worked on his book about the Lake District and the Fylde. He interviewed the shrimpers and the inshore fishermen who made a living from the sea. 'Old England' was then the oldest inhabitant who went down from the cliffs at low water, shrimping daily. Waugh tells of a fishing song written by William Garlick, a weaver of sail cloth known as 'pow davey'.

In the company of Old England Waugh caught whelks (sea-water snails). About this time, tons of cockles and shrimps were netted from Mussel Rock. The saying 'Owd (old) England' was what the farmers meant by boulder clay, reached when digging the top layers of sand. The three ancient settlements of Bispham, Norbreck and Thornton throughout the ages have been closely interwoven with the land and sea. It is surprising that such small settlements managed to be almost entirely self-supporting for years. The Red Banks or cliffs at Bispham were washed into the sea over the ages but the bases of these cliffs could still be found, outside a Norbreck Hotel, until erased by sea defence building.

CHAPTER 9

TORENTUM, CLEVELAS, ANGERSHOLME

—◈◈◈—

'THAT LONG, NARROW TRACT OF LITTLE MORE THAN SAND
CONTAINED BETWEEN THE RIVER WYRE AND THE IRISH CHANNEL.'

This is how the area of Thornton and Rossall was described by the Reverend St Vincent
Beechey and revealed in sketches made by Captain William Latham when he sailed up
the River Wyre in 1817. Two sketches in particular from his 'Looking Down the River
Wyre' show Rossall Hall, the great house of the Lord of the Manor, which faced a small
community of whitewashed buildings. Beyond rolled acres of treeless pasture broken only
by small farms. Most of the land was less than 25ft above sea level so the prevailing westerly
winds blowing relentlessly from the sea bent the stunted hedges and frequently caused
flooding of the whole area.

Marram grass covered the sandhills which were also starred with sea pinks, sea
holly, sea lavender and evening primrose. The main inhabitants were rabbits, hares,
herring gulls and oystercatchers in their thousands. The old wooden landmark which
was destroyed on a number of occasions by encroaching seas rose starkly against what
William Latham terms 'the Northern Mountains' (Bleasdale and the Lake District fells).
In those days there was a wealth of fish in the sea and many a Thornton, Norbreck and
Angersholme man went fishing and cockling. The Reverend John Thornber describes
the tremendous variety of sea shells 'pink and lilac in colour ... pearly trochuses, sea
worms, sea urchins, all kinds of sea weed ...'

Inland the flatness of the horizon was punctuated by Bourne Hall built on a drumlin,
and the tall windmill tower of Marsh Mill. Beyond the waste of Thornton Marsh
loomed the steel-blue hulk of Bleasdale Fells.

Thornton was recorded in the Domesday survey as Torentum. From early days its flat
plain was celebrated for oats and corn. In the eighteenth century grain was conveyed
by pack horses to markets in Poulton and Preston. Tied on a wooden saddle, the load

was firmly fixed with a 'wantah'. The leading horse was fitted with a bell and the team became so familiar with the route that the driver left them to find their way back to Thornton whilst he bargained over the load of grain delivered.

Bold Fleetwood Hesketh, Peter Hesketh Fleetwood's uncle, was a gentleman farmer. He enclosed Thornton Marsh, improved the land and increased productivity so much that the area became known as the cornfield of Amounderness. The promontory of Agmund was its original name, but as many as twelve variations of the ancient name have been traced. Splendid crops were grown all around Marsh Mill and in fields extending to the fertile banks of the River Wyre. Of the many farms that sprang up, including Marsh Farm, Rowland's, Cockle Hall and Hardman's, Burn Hall was the largest with over 355 acres. Field names reflect a sense of humour: Sea Sick; Salt Cote Hay; Cockle Meadow; Old Earth; Stoney Hill; Purgatory Meadow; Briary Field; Kipperbone.

Thornton Marsh or 'Common Waste' separated the sea from the river and flooding was a problem.

Under the Marsh Act Award of 1805 Bold Fleetwood Hesketh tried to keep the sea from his fertile land. He built the high bank of gravel over Thornton Marsh which became the now familiar Victoria Road. However, at the equinox the sea still reached Parr's Lane, now Meadows Avenue. Because of this, Adam Parr, who lived in a thatched cottage, managed to get his annual rent reduced from £14 to £12. Mr Holden, a Methodist Preacher, had other problems. He complained: 'I was sorely tried by the people of Thornton Marsh. They did not wish to be converted.' However, the twentieth century heralded in the popular Wignall Memorial Methodist Church on Victoria Road East.

Old Cleveleys or Clevelas had little more than the Cleveleys Hotel whose landlord, Robert Hindle, was instrumental in saving the crew of the New Brunswick barque *Abana* in December 1894. During that storm eight vessels were wrecked in Morecambe Bay, an oyster stall landed on the roof of Blackpool Central Station, Thornton lost haystacks and Marsh Mill sails were damaged.

Two views of the *Riverdance Ferry* from Ireland, wrecked off Angersholme and Clevelas, 31 December 2008. (E. Ramsey)

As the century advanced and Thornton became Thornton-Cleveleys, the thatched cottages and early brick buildings along Victoria Road, originally called Ramper Road, were converted into shops. Shops! Mr Shawcross, 'high class confectioner'; Robert Hodgson, hairdresser and tobacconist, 'dealer in English and foreign cigars'; W.E. Bulley, fruiterer and greengrocer, and many others run by high-sounding traders.

A cab and taxi-cab proprietor catered for weddings but was also a 'general courier'. Woodbine Cottage, visited regularly by the famous nineteenth-century orator and politician John Bright, with the coming of the motor age was knocked down and made into a garage. Sophistication greeted the shoals of elderly folk who retired to fashionable Thornton-Cleveleys.

Posters for Libby's fruit salads and Edwards desiccated soups (sold in quarter, half and one pound canisters and one ounce packets) were advertised on the walls of grocers' shops like H.B. Shepherd who also declaimed that:

> There are several kinds of Irish bacon but if you want the very best Irish roll, go to H.B. Shepherd, wholesale and retail grocer, who sells nothing but the best – also our Lancashire cheese is REAL Lancashire not American and is made in the Fylde district.

Everything in clothing was available in Victoria Road from Bradock's 'Stand Hard suits for rough boys' to delicate Bangkok straw hats for the ladies. A herbalist sold worm powder, nerve powder, fever cure, pile powders, indigestion mixture and stomach bitters. Miss L. Glaister of Beach Road told me that the tiny shop smelled wonderful from its mixture of tinctures and sweet herbs. The lady who ran it gave customers her recipe for Beef and Malt Wine:

> 1 pint of old port wine, 1 ounce of beef extract and 4 ounces of malt extract, with instructions to mix the above and keep well corked for about seven days, occasionally shaking.

Thornton shopkeepers were regular orators and even poets, advertising in rhyme: 'This is a shop for a pot and a pan, A place for a jug and a kettle. But if there's nothing you want to buy, Please bring us something to fettle' (fettle = mend).

It is hard to believe that the area where we now enjoy shopping was originally open free pasture on which any cottager could keep geese or cattle. There were no public roads, just ancient winding track ways, the shape of which can still be seen in the country lane running from Whiteholme to Carleton. More poetry follows: 'Relish those rolling names on ancient maps by which this wild, windswept area of sand and shingle was once known –Torentum, Clevelas and Angersholme!'

CHAPTER 10

MANCHESTER

Extensive railway systems existed at both Manchester and Liverpool Docks, essential links with mercantile fleets. SS *Manchester Mariner* awaits a train of cargo for Montreal in 1966. The shunting engine in use, MSC 32, a Hudswell Clarke 0-6-0T built in 1903, was one of the last three steam locomotives in use there. Soon after this photograph was taken it was withdrawn, having worked a total of 300,000 hours on the dock. The construction of the East Lancashire road in the 1920s and the opening of the Mersey Tunnel in 1934 brought Manchester and Liverpool closer. Canals also linked an intricate network of communication vital to a port's trade, one of the best examples being the Manchester Ship Canal opened in 1894.

A bold Victorian engineering feat, a continuation of the Mersey waterway bringing American commerce into the heart of an important inland city, Mr Daniel Adamson's project gave Manchester the position of fourth port in Great Britain. In its report of 1924 the Manchester Ship Canal, constituting the port of Manchester, was stated to be 36 miles in length with a 28ft depth of water. Vessels of 15,000 tons plied from the sea on regular, frequent steamship services. There were fifty-three hydraulic, seventy-three steam and 130 electric cranes in a dock area of 406 acres. The terminal facilities were unequalled in the world. Number 9 dock's two elevators with a combined capacity of 3 million bushels could be filled at the rate of 900 tons an hour whilst ships were discharging general cargo. This indicates how busy the port of Manchester was when it was judged the most efficient in Europe by an American engineer. By 1959 it was the third largest port, having initiated a modernisation programme including 200 miles of track to Ellesmere Port, replacing steam with diesel. Times here have also changed and present trade is with Europe, notably Spain. 19 million pounds of E.E.C. money was needed to form a marina and to keep the great volume of water flowing if only for the safety of nearby Warrington lying at sea level. Such large grain ships as the *Arklow Royal* ideally need a pilot on board. October 1987 brought the news that the

The Manchester Ship Canal, 1900. (Author's collection)

The Bulls Head, thought to be Manchester's oldest inn. On the night that the city was visited by the German Luftwaffe in 1940, Ye Olde Wellington Inn, built in the fifteenth century, was left standing in the midst of ruins. (Author's collection)

Above left: Manchester New Dock, *c.*1920. (Author's collection)

Above right: The Free Trade Hall, December 1940, after the bombing. Trade between the cities of Manchester and Liverpool was damaged. (Author's collection)

link between Manchester City Council and the Manchester Ship Canal was to end, the city fathers to receive 7 million pounds but no longer to serve as directors. Even before 1820 Warrington, though not strictly a port, by virtue of the rivers Mersey and Irwell had many advantages of commerce. The town, which grew up near the ford of the river, manufactured sailcloth, developing as a port in the eighteenth century. The Warrington Academy became well known for its scholarship. James Baines wrote in 1825: 'The communication between Manchester and Liverpool is incessant; the brick dust coloured sails of the barges are seen every hour of the day on their passage. The prosperity of Wigan has also been advanced by its inland navigation.'

MANCHESTER SHIP CANAL

Although it is no longer considered an important shipping route, six million tonnes of freight are carried annually. The canal is owned by Peel Ports who also own the Port of Liverpool. Salford Docks used to serve as an unloading place but more usually now various places alongside the canal are used. Grain ships still go to the Rank Hovis mill at Trafford Park.

Many ships are now too large to navigate the canal but it is interesting to note that in 2007 Tesco began to use the canal for transporting wine between Liverpool and Irlam Container. Here cargo is off-loaded and taken to a bottling plant nearby which saves 700,000 road haulage miles each year.

CHAPTER 11

PRESTON

—◦◦◦—

Although there are references to ships at Preston as early as 1360 they were of small tonnage. In the seventeenth century it was reported that: 'The river is much choaked up with sand' and indeed the Ribble with its uncertain channels and 'infernal banks' continued to give trouble. Between 1838 and 1853 a second Ribble Navigation Company was formed. John Woodburn, Mayor, with his family attended a ceremony at the bottom of a coffer dam and a 12hp dredger, the wooden hull for which was made at Speakman's Yard, Fishergate Lane. Training walls were constructed using the stone excavated for the dam. These improvements whereby many vessels could proceed direct to Preston lessened the need for Lytham dock but events like the Christmas hurricane of 1852, a year when earthquakes were experienced in Lancashire, did not help. The Preston Pilot reported that the sea rushed past the Regatta Inn on the riverside for 60 yards up Fishergate and for miles the Ribble overflowed its banks, sinking fishing and pleasure boats, some being carried into fields on the flood tide.

Preston dock was once the largest single dock in the country, and opened originally in 1903. The steam yacht *Aline* entered, dressed overall, and a special *Preston Herald* supplement was printed when on 25 June 1892 HRH Duke of Edinburgh, later Edward VII, performed the ceremony.

There were however, red faces in Preston. Adequate equipment – coal hoists, cranes, capstans were missing and the channel from the sea was again giving trouble. In that year Pictorial England and Wales called Preston 'a port of some consequence, an important place, favoured with 15 distinct royal charters.' The view from the lock gates shows Maudland church spire, the Harris Library and Museum and many tall factory chimneys. Making a viable port continued to be a costly, seemingly never-ending task of maintaining training walls, tipping and dredging. To house the tipper a fixed lighthouse on piles was erected on the north wall 12 miles from the dock, safer than Ansdell gas buoy and the Gut gas buoy which required large containers. Channels changed their courses continually, until the light that emitted from the lighthouse was burned out, but it did all the same lessen the terrors of the Ribble. One hundred years earlier a man from Guides Inn on the Ribble shore had to row out in a boat to refill warning lamps with paraffin. Traffic volume continued to increase: 95,000 tons in 1893, 220,000 in 1894, but so did silting, causing vessels which tried to achieve the impossible to ground. Suction sand pumps, hoppers and inevitable litigation added to the expense. In recent years the struggle has been given up and the docks closed but a new lease of life beckons. Grants of over £12 million pounds have been made to give impetus to a scheme which should eventually offer housing, commerce, light industry and leisure facilities. Already functioning at this 400-acre site and having also taken on a new lease of life is *Manxman*. An historic ship of the Isle of Man Steam Packet Company, overall length 344ft, she was launched on 8 February 1955 and in service for twenty-seven years during which time she carried 2 million passengers to such ports as Dublin, Heysham, Fleetwood, Liverpool, Workington and Barrow. With 2,200 capacity, she cost £847,000, the last of a class of six ships which were necessary replacements after the Second World War. At the end of 1981 speculation was that she would follow her sister ship *Mona's Isle* to the breaker's yard. On her last sailing that season *Manxman* carried only 490 passengers. Her final voyage was made between Liverpool and Douglas on 4 September 1982.

This, Europe's last remaining steam-powered passenger liner, was for a time moored at Preston and used for all manner of functions such as a film set for *Chariots of Fire* and *The Missionary*. The breaker's yard was the be its last stop, but enthusiasts still wish to preserve the *Manxman*.

Preston was once a thriving inland port but part of the old port is now being redeveloped. It was a centre for cotton spinning for 150 years and remains an important place of trade and business being an important railway junction halfway between London and Scotland. Bronze Age burial urns and coins, part of a Viking treasure hoard, were found buried near the ford across the River Ribble. Its history goes far back in time. It has the right since the thirteenth century to hold a Merchant Guild under Henry II Charter in 1179. The Guild has been celebrated (apart from during the First World War) every twenty years since 1542.

The barque *Clara* was wrecked on her way to Preston from Norway in December 1906, a trip she had made on twenty-four occasions without mishap. This 430-ton wooden barque was built in 1857 at the port of Miramichi and was captained by Olaf Peterson. Carrying 56 tons of wooden deals, she had tried unsuccessfully to obtain a pilot 1 mile south of Nelson Buoy. At midnight her keel struck bottom in the midst of a sudden, fierce squall.

Under the continual bumping, a portion of the rudder broke and her main topmast crashed carrying away the sails. Fearing capsize, the crew took to the ship's boat but were blown helplessly over sandbanks until the Fleetwood lifeboat saved them at 8a.m. Hundreds had gathered, alerted by the lifeboat gun's signal, to watch the drama.

Above left: The wreck of *Furu* or *Old Hunter*. (Author's collection)

Above right: Preston Port, the Town Hall, burned down in the late 1940s. (Author's collection)

A similar barque to *Clara* of 545 tons, the *Henrietta* more than fifty years before had the same experience. She was sailing between Liverpool and the Nigerian slave trade port of Bonny. Her captain was Mels Peter Jacobson, born 1815, the son of a Danish sea captain, who was paid £15 a month by Lovatt & Corran of Liverpool. The *Henrietta* had tried to help the *Laura Campbell* which had lost her main mast and sails in a December gale. According to the *Liverpool Telegraph* letters and wreckage from the *Henrietta* were washed up a number of weeks later in January 1851. Captain Jacobson and crew were all presumed lost at sea.

Chapter 12

Poulton-Le-Fylde, Wardleys and Skippool

—⧸∞⧹—

POULTON (LATER TO BE CALLED POULTON-LE FYLDE)

For centuries Poulton was a port of importance having two harbours, Wardleys on the east bank of the Wyre and Skippool on the west. Ships called with flax and tallow from Russia, brought in by merchants William and James Blackburn as early as 1590. Oranges and sugar came from the West Indies, timber and iron from the Baltic. Flax from Belfast and grain from Scotland were still being unloaded in the 1880s, with Poulton and Garstang cheeses travelling coastwise on return.

All the mediaeval appurtenances of an ancient market town shown in the photographs overleaf include the stocks, broken down by passing traffic when the motor age arrived. A few yards from these stocks in 1708, in a house in the square lived the customs officers. William Jennings received £30 per annum and the five others shared £70 between them. Facing the stocks, at the rear of Mr Harrison's dwelling, forty people from the Poor House laboured at flax dressing and twine spinning; in Sandy Lane was a rope walk and the area once called Angell's Holme, on the tributary leading to Skippool, had been used for boat building since the days of Elizabeth I. Between 1806 and 1808, 500 tons of limestone came from Ulverston and 9,000 quarters of oats from Dumfries and Whitehaven. Coal was unloaded from Preston. Another legal landing place near Poulton was Mains Brow where ships anchored close to the banks, settling on mud and gravel as the tide went out, only to refloat on the next. Merchant John Bourne landed timber on his Stalmine estate, to float it, chained to Wardleys where the barque *Hope*, 415 tons, was built by Matthew Lewtas and lost at sea in 1862. A warehouse was built at Skippool in 1741 for the West Indies trade: tobacco, sugar, rum. Wardleys, referred to as 'a small seaport on the Wyre', had a stone wharf and four warehouses.

As trade declined, the warehouses, now demolished, were used as shippons, receptacles for guano manure and agricultural produce. Even after the Customs had been removed

Above left: The author conducting a Town Trail in June 1991 of the ancient Market Town mentioned in the Domesday Book. (Author's collection)

Above right: Morris dancing, Church Street, Poulton, taken summer 2001. (Author's collection)

Above left: Snowdrops and crocuses in Poulton churchyard, that people come for miles to photograph. Taken spring 2003. (Author's collection)

Above right: Joseph, grandson of the author, by Poulton Stocks, seated on Market Cross Steps in June 2005. (Author's collection)

to Fleetwood in 1839 Wardleys, then a sub-port under Preston, remained a legal quay. Poulton was under the port of Chester in George I's reign when commissioners appointed 'places, quays and wharves for the landing, discharging, lading or shipping of merchandise.' When Poulton was called 'the Metropolis of the Fylde' fourteen inns, including the Ship Inn with its original sign of a full-rigged sailing ship, indicated its importance as market town and port. Sailors lodged in Pott's Entry, now fashionable Chapel Street Walks, where many fights equalled Blackpool's 'rowdy Sundays'. Until the Act of Liberation, 1833, some north-west inland mills used slave labour: the large worsted mill at Dolphinholme which made top hats and the silk mill at Galgate. Slaves were landed at Greenodd for sale to rich Lake District houses where, as in London, it was fashionable to have a 'blackamoor' in the household. As the *Liverpool Advertiser* reveals, because port dues were cheaper, Poulton along with Preston sent ships to the colonies for the purchase of slaves. One entry shows that the ships *Betty* and *Martha*, owned by Kirkham merchants Langton, Shepherd and Birley, bought sixty-five slaves at Sierra Leone, but in 1761 slaves got the upper hand on board the *Mary* of Lancaster, murdering all the crew.

Poulton as a port died completely after Fleetwood was built. At one time in the eighteenth century, Poulton was attached to the Port of Chester perhaps because flooding could be a problem when equinoctial tides swept in up the River Wyre to Wardleys and Skippool. However, the Customs Officer whom it is known was paid £30 per year during Queen Anne's reign had his place of business in the square at Poulton until 1840, when Stephen Burridge was transferred to Fleetwood.

Church of St Chad, Poulton-le-Fylde. The rounded apse was added in 1868. (Ted Ramsey, 2000)

In a letter from Preston one visitor stated 'Poulton was once a port of eminence but has now lapsed into seven sleepy streets'. Another account from Hull said much the same but embellished Poulton's market square with a duck pond. The halcyon days of trade to and from Skippool, when oranges, tallow, flax for Birley's mill in Kirkham and American grain for Mr Parkinson's flour mill in Poulton were over.

A rope walk flourished in Sandy Lane, Poulton, until the 1860s when a local townsman reported, 'The Rope Works is doing well.'

Fleetwood's cargo trade was also busy. Canvas and rope would still be in demand and Fleetwood's Timber Pond handled planks and beams from Norway.

SKIPPOOL

This curious name is written on ancient maps as 'Skippon', a name that may have been derived from the skipps of the Saxons. Richard Seed was an important shipper at Skippool in the nineteenth century handling cargoes of slate and coal. On the opposite bank at Wardleys Mr R. Silcock started a bone manure works about the same time.

1956 photograph of Wardleys Creek, early port for Poulton. (Author's collection)

Above left: Wardleys Creek, Poulton 2010. (Sheila Isherwood)

Above right: Skippool Creek, August 2010. (Sheila Isherwood)

Wardley's ferry and port had warehouses. Sailing ships unloaded cargoes of oranges, tallow and flax in the sixteenth century. The Blackburn brothers of Thistleton grew rich. Further up river stood Cockle Hall owned by Peter Hesketh. This cottage passed to his second wife Virginie and then to his son Louis. To get the ferryman, travellers rang a bell and whistled. Mrs Isherwood told me about one of the last crossings, when a swift tide was sweeping in from the sea and rocking the boat alarmingly.

When Mr Lewtas built the barque *Hope* in 1830 it proved to be the largest ever vessel built on the River Wyre. As the ship glided into the water near Cockle Hall river water flooded Skippool Road as far as Bleasdale's Cottages. The crowds were drenched all except the people who had arrived in bathing vans from Blackpool. The day had been declared a holiday, being regarded by one and all as a great event.

WARDLESS AND SKIPPOLE

The well-known historian Edward Baines in his Gazeteer of Lancashire, 1801, referred to Wardless as a small seaport on the River Wyre where vessels of 300 tons burden could unload: 'At present Poulton is a creek under Preston despite Wardless and Skippole being viable landing places for sea-going vessels.' Situated 4 miles from Poulton-in-the-Fylde, 'a place of great antiquity', lived the principal coast officer James Bisbrowne in Market Place. Along with other seamen he pointed out the safety of the River Wyre and the drawback of not having a bridge across it.

Sections from early Ordnance Survey maps (1848-1915) show proof of these small ports now faded into history, the fate that befell Sunderland Point (as will be seen in chapter 22); sailors from this once useful small port, in its decline, called it Cape Famine and 'the deserted village'.

One O.S. print shows Wardleys Ferry near Wardleys Hotel. The name 'Pool' was then widely used for anchorages as evidenced in Skippool, Skippool Bridge and Pool Side House. Shard House and Shard Ferry pre-date Shard Bridge built in 1864. Skippspool Bridge was reported to be in ruinous state in 1702. £25 had to be collected by James Pawson, Thomas Walmsley and Richard Breckell to repair it.

A manuscript from 1786 reveals that the Bridge Inn at Shard was once the original Ferry Boat House. There were so many ferries over the Wyre and crossing in small boats could be hazardous in stormy weather. Rushes grew down to the river's edge and this same 1786 document reveals that before Shard Bridge was built, there was an oil lamp used as a guide light for rowing boats crossing to the opposite side and a warning not to proceed down river towards the sea. The Parish church of St Chad has an account of two brothers from Skippool who drowned in the River Wyre one stormy night in August 1828 – Joseph and Richard Wilding.

By 1954 Skippool Creek had a cafe and was attracting 'dry land sailors' with its marina. At this point the River Skipton entered the Wyre, draining from Marton Mere. Opposite was Wardleys, Poulton port's second harbour where the sixteenth- and seventeenth-century Russian ships called. In the eighteenth century there was an arrangement with a Mr Rhoe to supply ships for the Tsar of Russia but instead of building new ships, Rhoe refurbished old ones and soon the Russians ceased trading.

Fleetwood became active in 1840 but even after the removal of the Customs House from Poulton to Fleetwood, Wardleys remained a legal quay. As many as seven ships

Above: Skippool Creek, Poulton 2010. (Author's collection)

Right: The Lewtas family. Mr M. Lewtas, shipbuilder, at Wardleys, his wife, two sons and housekeeper pictured in 1873. He built the barque *Hope* (415 tons) there, the first Wardleys vessel to enter Shanghai. (Author's collection)

China clay from Fowey in Cornwall was brought by schooner to the ports of Wardleys and Skippool. They returned with cheeses from the Fylde of Lancashire – 'A schooner leaves harbour'. (© Claire Sellick, Celtic Scene, Fowey)

On the jetty near Cockle Hall where you waved and whistled for the Rowing Boat to come across to take you to Wardleys, 1963. (Sheila Isherwood)

Skippool Creek.
(Sheila Isherwood)

Suction pump dredger *Poulton* and crew, 1901, a twin-screwed vessel built at Paisley in 1899, operated in the channel of the River Wyre and beyond Wyre Light. John R. Wright (2nd left, front row) was mate and later became skipper. The dredger *Bleesdale* in 1968 recovered a Mediterranean vessel lost from a sailing ship in 1860 and a bronze cannon. (Author's collection)

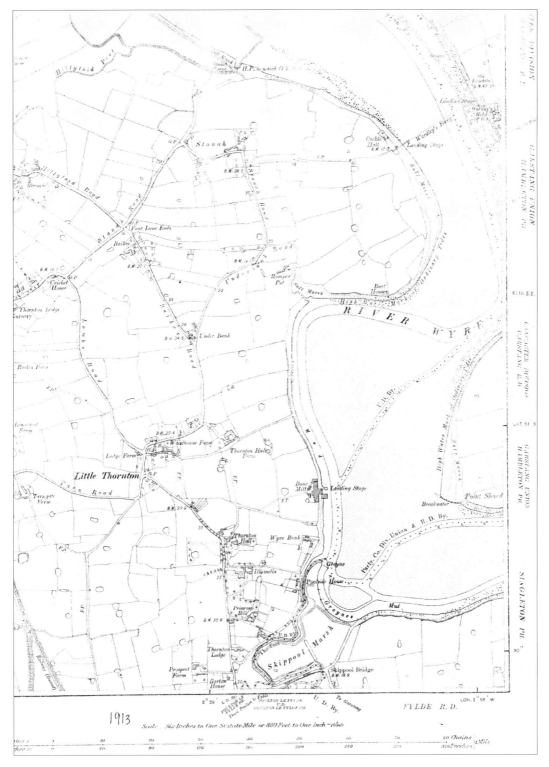

1913

Scale... Six Inches to One Statute Mile or 880 Feet to One Inch = 1:10560

The Bone Mill with its landing stage is shown above Skippool Marsh on this Ordnance Survey
section, 1913. (Author's collection)

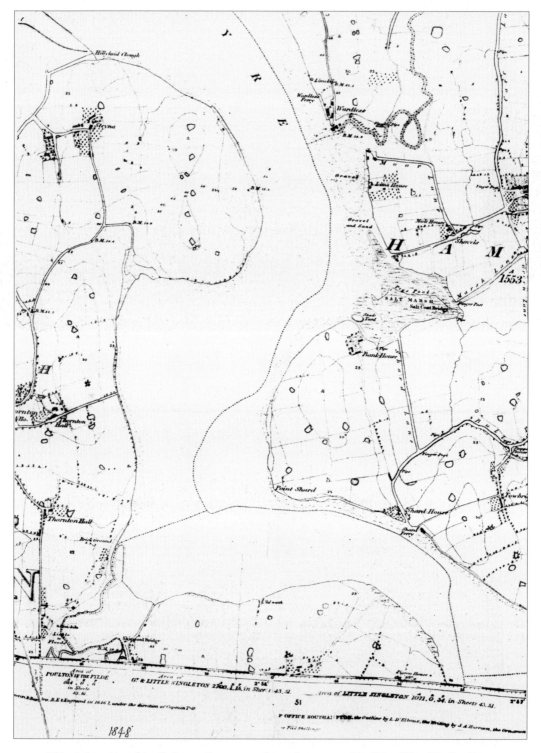

This 1848 section of the Ordnance Survey map shows the course of the River Wyre, Wardless Ferry, Saltcoats, Point Shard and Stena (Stannah). (Author's collection)

Above left: Market Steps Poulton and Cross. To the left of the photograph were the premises of the officers of Customs; Stephen Burridge was in charge until 1839 when he moved to Fleetwood. (Author's collection)

Above right: Today's scene looking towards ICI from Stannah on River Wyre. (Author's collection)

Wardleys Cottage where William Swarbrick lived. For fifty years he ferried between Cockle Hall and Wardleys. Born in 1816, William also ferried the first loads of gravel for the building of Fleetwood. (Author's collection)

A view of Wardleys Hotel. (Author's collection)

could arrive. Swainsons and Birleys of Kirkham had their own quays where flax from Russia and later Ireland was unloaded.

Skippool was also known in the seventeenth century for harbouring a witch. William Wilson denounced Dorothie Shaw on 12 September 1627: 'Thou art a witch and a demdyke,' but Dorothie denied it before magistrate Richard Burgh of Larbreck. A ducking-stool was kept at the bottom of Breck for suspected witches and nagging wives.

Fords over the River Wyre are mentioned in Indentures as early as 1330 – Aldwath, Shard and Ford of Bulk, Larbreck Hall and Cartford. The Romans may have had a lower ford that ran from Min End (mouth of the Wyre) towards Preesall Hill. Shard was in use for hundreds of years, important because it was on a highroad where the river is 500 yards wide. Old Shard Inn stood on the right bank and Shard Hotel on the left.

It is thought that the Saxons used Skippool Creek. (There was a group of Saxon fishermen who worked from Cross Slack, Lytham.) Richard Seed, an important shipper in the nineteenth century, brought cargoes of slate and coal to Skippool whilst Mr R. Silcock on the opposite bank set up a bone manure works (shown on the Ordnance Survey section). Seventeenth-century Skippool was a favourite haunt of the gentry for cockfighting but the twentieth century has turned it into a modern marina.

Poulton was originally a 'pool village'. Pool also features in Pilling, the Celtic *pyll* meaning pool or creek.

CHAPTER 13

FLEETWOOD

⟝ᴥ⟞

'THE WIRE IS A GOOD, SAFE RIVER' PORT FLEETWOOD

'The survey of Morecambe Bay is entirely charged in the accounts but two thirds of the cost will be defrayed by Sir Hesketh Fleetwood, our worthy Chairman, who in this as in several other instances spontaneously offered to relieve the Company's expenditure.' This survey, done by Captain Henry Mangles Denham, who was employed to improve the harbour, is referred to in the October 1842 Report of Friederick Cortazzi, Managing Director of the Board of the Preston and Wyre Railway Harbour and Dock Company. The original idea was that the improving of the harbour should be run as a separate undertaking but railway building troubles led to the amalgamation of both companies in the Act of 1839.

The Lords of the Admirality first sent Captain Belcher, hydrographer, to survey; his proposals being published in the Nautical Magazine of 1837. One of his ideas was to construct a pier from the Mount but the recommendations of Denham were finally adopted. Improvement of the harbour and the inauguration of a Steam Navigation Service were vital to the success of the port but money troubles stunted the full ripeness of the scheme. Owing to some loss of confidence, dock shares were not taken up as rapidly as was hoped. A true dock was not to come until 1877 but Peter's struggle to implement the original plan and bolster finances from his own pocket was yet again illustrative of his optimistic, enterprising Victorian spirit. Regular steam and rail services commenced the day after the opening of the Railway. In May 1841 *Fireking*, one of the finest and fastest steamers afloat, made the Fleetwood to Ardrossan run. Steamer services were operating to the Isle of Man and Belfast by 7 October. Paddle steamers plied daily to Ulverston for the Lake District and the first *Fleetwood Chronicle*, 11 November 1843, advertised 'Best Route to Belfast and Londonderry via Fleetwood. The North Lancashire Steam Navigation Company's iron steamers Prince of Wales

Steamboat Pier and Railway Station, Port Fleetwood, *c.*1890. (Author's collection)

Fleetwood Dock, 1910. The Timber Pond was used as a fish dock when cargo trade declined and Fleetwood became the third most important fishing port in Britain. (Author's collection)

and Princess Alice…For Londonderry the powerful steamer Robert Napier.' In the ensuing years, the servant appears to have ousted the master. Frederick Kemp owned the Steam Navigation Company and Peter was heavily in debt.

Aware of the needs of a growing town and port, Peter wrote many letters from Rossall Hall to the Lords Commissioners seeking approval for the bonding of goods in warehouses which he proposed to erect for tobacco and all East India goods besides making bonding arrangements for timber. He urged the removal of the main Customs house from Poulton to Fleetwood:

> I pray your Lordships will give direction for such removal as soon as the requisite building can be erected and which I am willing to build immediately, having ordered a plot of land to be staked out for the site of the Custom House and suitable residence for the Officers.

Permission was granted. The original Customs House was finished in 1840 and still exists. It became Fleetwood Town Hall. Doctor William Beattie, on his visit in 1842, commented on it and other Decimus Burton buildings, speaking lyrically of Fleetwood as 'this new Tyre'. The limits of the port were set out on vellum, a 'Plan of the Port of Fleetwood with the legal quays and wharfs setting forth the boundaries thereof.'

Fleetwood was made a Warehousing Port by Treasury order on 30 May 1839, 'a supernumerary port' but a rider was added, 'Should the communication by the Ribble to Preston be improved My Lords will be prepared to reconsider the whole arrangements.' The 'Master of Rossall' was accused of serving his own ends rather than those of his parliamentary constituency when Preston was relegated to a creek under Fleetwood. Once again the Preston press took up the warcry by viciously attacking 'Fleetwood's darling scheme of aggrandisement' and Peter was challenged to a duel by Colonel Yorke Scarlett, who backed MP Townley Parker's cries for the decision on the respective ports to be rescinded. Besides the Preston grumblings there were local complaints from John Bourne of Stalmine Hall and William Birley, flax merchant of Kirkham, who said that their properties were not within parliamentary limits and should be toll free. Did the improvements to the harbour justify the claim that Fleetwood stood on its own considerable merits and deserved the privileges granted? Captain Denham in his sailing directions pointed out that the River Wyre flowed in such a way as always to have a scouring effect on the river bed so that its natural basin, the Canshe Hole, was preserved. The river narrowed where the new wharves were being constructed and flowed so swiftly here that all the silt deposits were kept in suspension and swept out to Morecambe Bay, where cross currents from the River Lune carried the silt further, thus preventing a bar forming across the river mouth. At the entrance of the Wyre was placed the first lighthouse of its kind involving 'the application of Mitchell's ingenious mooring screw in submarine foundations,' far superior to a lightship which could break free in rough conditions. Wyre pilot boats of sloop and yawl rig cruised

Above: Fleetwood – *Maude Pickup* Lifeboat 1894–1930. (Author's collection)

Below left: Portus Setantiorum – possible site of the ancient Roman port which became Fleetwood. This is one of a group, including the town surveyor, Mr Melville, inspecting for evidence *c.*1975. (Author's collection)

Below right: Fleetwood Freeport visitors in 1989. Left to right: Jocelyn, Catherine, Eddie. (Author's collection)

between Formby and Haverigg Points. 'Happily for the mariner and this new Port enterprise few directions will be necessary to enable even a stranger to enter it. In thick weather you can feel your way.' The new screw-pile lighthouse arrived on the schooner *Collingue* from Belfast on 26 November 1839 and was erected within a day 2 miles offshore. That Peter met the blind engineer is evidence by a letter written on 28 November. 'I saw the gentleman stone blind at Captain Denham's, who has built a lighthouse. It is beautiful to watch his intelligent countenance and he feels as proud of having invented what saves life as on account of its cleverness. How thankful did I feel to merciful God who when he took away one left one eye to me.'

Mitchell used to work singing alongside his men encouraging their labours. He felt the structure of the lighthouse with his sensitive hands and it is said that, working over it, he detected a flaw which to the sighted had passed unnoticed. Together with the two stone lighthouses designed by Decimus Burton it shone forth on 1 December 1840 at the ceremony marking the opening of the Cut Channel to night traffic. The moment of unmasking must have been wonderful to the man whose money and enterprise had made it possible and also to the crowds who had gathered on the shores. As night descended Sir Peter, in company with other ladies and gentlemen, embarked in a steamer navigated by Captain Denham. The boom of cannon mingled with cheers. Rockets soared aloft, though the rejoicing was short-lived. Records show that money was insufficient. Dock gates were opposed on grounds of cost. One steam dredger was lost on the way to Fleetwood and the formation of a Tontine Company to boost the undertaking was by no means an unqualified success. This aimed to assist the Chartered Company for the construction of docks and warehouses but the Directors expressed concern at the small number of shares subscribed for. At this point it seemed wise to unite Railway and Harbour with Dock.

George Stephenson's Report in 1839 had recommended that a quay large enough to accommodate three steam vessels be constructed and the result was a sturdy piece of Victorian Engineering 600ft long, completed in 1841 and similar to the Brunswick Pier at the terminus of Blackwall Railway. Whilst the railway was the means of supplying timber, coal, cotton, flax, butter, milk and eggs to Preston and beyond, trade with Ireland through the new port could make meat and poultry available at a cheaper rate than via Liverpool, some of those whose trade Peter hoped to capture for his New Liverpool. 'Fired with the exhorbitant charges at Liverpool, the merchants of Manchester have turned their eyes to Fleetwood,' printed the *Fleetwood Chronicle* on 5 October 1845. In the same year the Tidal Commissioners praised the harbour improvements, forecasting a thriving port on the evidence of S.P. Bidder, Frederick Kemp and Robert Gerrard; the latter a pilot of twenty years' experience who, knowing both Lune and Wyre, stated, 'Vessels have often to remain at anchor near the foot of Wyre before they can get up to Glasson Dock. That is never the case with Fleetwood. There is not the least difficulty in taking the harbour by day or night.' Belfast traders preferred Wyre to Preston because 'the former was at once open to the sea.'

Above left: The Freeport at Fleetwood is built where the docks were transformed into a large, modern marina. (Author's collection)

Above right: The Mayor and Mayoress of Fleetwood with Mr Lionel Marr arriving for the launch of Catherine Rothwell's book *Fleetwood: A Pictorial History* on board the preserved stern trawler *Jacinta*. November 2005. (Author's collection)

Shipwrecked sailors landed at Fleetwood from the wreck of *Old Hunter*, 1906. (Author's collection)

Jacinta Stern Trawler, Fleetwood Dock, taken on 31 October 2007. (Christopher Ramsey)

The double-headed eagle, part of Peter Hesketh's crest and the Fleetwood family coat of arms. (Author's collection)

150 years ago when Fleetwood-on-Wyre rose from a waste of sandhills it was aptly described as 'a beautiful town from the wilderness won'. Peter Hesketh, Lord of the Manor, who had inherited coastline from Formby Point to mouth of Wyre, conceived the daring plan of building a seaside resort alongside a thriving port to handle commerce from Ireland, Scotland and the seven seas. With acres of land and a river shaped by nature for this purpose the plan was sound but too ambitious. Fleetwood commenced as a port in 1839, with customs established by order of Treasury, a ruling relegating Preston to creek under Fleetwood, which outraged that proud town, but by 1844 the decision was reversed. Although Fleetwood regained her independence five years later, Customs moved to a modest building which an 1898 photograph shows as Customs Watch House, boarding station for ships entering the port. Cut into its supporting sandstone blocks, L.Q. (Legal Quay) can still be seen. From this point crowds of people used to watch Mr Stoba starting the once-famous regattas.

The three-masted ship *Valkyrien*, 1902, and others positioned on the 'Gridiron' where ships were repaired. (Author's collection)

The launching of *Harriet*, now preserved as the last and oldest fishing smack. The little girl (centre front) is Harriet Leadbetter; the fishing boat was named after her. (Author's collection)

Part of the Fleetwood fleet of fishing smacks, 1902. (Author's collection)

Jacinta, stern trawler, preserved at Heritage Centre, Wyre Dock, 2007. (Author's collection)

Above: The *Duke of Connaught* packet boat worked the designated Royal Mail Route from Fleetwood to Belfast and Londonderry, after the Government arranged, in 1850, for the conveyance of mail by sea. (Author's collection)

Left: Custom House, built 1838 by architect Sir Decimus Burton. The building is now Fleetwood Museum. (Author's collection)

The 2010 ferry from Knott End approaches Fleetwood. (Author's collection)

The *Sceptre*. Some of these early fishing boats would still use a sail to 'speed the craft'. Prejudice against steampower was evident as sailing boats when fitted with engines were not always shown to be suitable. The *Sceptre* belonged to the Clifton Fishing Company. (Author's collection)

Coronation festivities at Fleetwood in 1911 – a model of the famous fishing boat *Harriet* on Mr M. Rawcliffe's coal cart, part of the Coronation procession in 1911. (Author's collection)

A Moody and Kelly vessel, possibly *New Crown*, moored alongside GY369. Four-masted barques brought wheat for the grain elevator. From San Francisco came *Henrietta*, *Loanda* and *Attilio*. (Author's collection)

The wreck of the *Old Hunter* off the coast of Shell Wharf in 1906. Rights from wreck of the sea were due to the Lord of the Manor, or later to the Fleetwood Estate Company. The wreck happened one fiercely windy day during Fylde's typically stormy winter on 20 February 1906. (Sketch by John Charles Houghton)

One of Fleetwood's first Trinity House pilots was a local man whose vellum certificate, granted 17 May 1855, states:

> Know ye that William Swarbrick who is at present Master of the ship Flying Dutchman has been examined as to his fitness to pilot Royal Consort, 303 tons, Prince of Wales, 312 tons, Princess Alice, 257 tons, within the following limits from the sea and out of harbour west along the coast from Formby Point to West Havering port of Duddon.

William, who also took the lifeboats out by steam tug on the Wyre on stormy nights, had this certificate renewed annually for twenty years.

Certificate issued to Henry Joel Snasdell after passing an examination on seamanship at Fleetwood, 19 March 1913. (Author's collection)

CHAPTER 14

JOHN GIBSON – MASTER SHIPBUILDER

A member of one of the best known and respected families of nineteenth-century Fleetwood, John Gibson became one of the town's most famous shipbuilders. Born in Kirkaldy in 1815, the year of Waterloo, he came to Fleetwood at the age of twenty-two to work on the pile-driving which was essential in the construction of the Preston and Wyre railway. John lodged at the nearest place available, 'Twenty Houses', Burn Naze, which a hundred years later became the site of ICI. From here he tramped to work every morning across the sandy peninsula, always within sound of the sea.

John was soon to make his mark. In 1846 the *Fleetwood Chronicle* reported that he chaired a meeting held at the Fleetwood Arms to discuss a testimonial to Henry Smith, a pioneer who worked so hard to keep the Preston and Wyre Railway going throughout the difficult years and established Fleetwood as a Packet Station for carrying the Royal Mail to Belfast.

John's first shipyard was near the old fish warehouse, from where vessels were dragged across the quay and launched by being dropped broadside into the river. From here he moved to opposite Queen's Terrace where he built a patent slipway. By 1857 he had formed a partnership with James Butcher which was to last for three years. Fishing smacks *Surprise*, *Cygnet*, *Ellen* and *Ann* were the first to be built for Meols fishermen who, on Sir Peter Hesketh's Fleetwood's invitation, had settled in Fleetwood when tides at Southport began to recede. When the partnership was dissolved James Butcher retained the block-making interest, which John later took over on Mr Butcher's death.

By 1861 the shipyard of John Gibson and Sons was sited where the P&O Ferries now dock. The Fleetwood Improvement Commissioners received complaints from Queen's Terrace residents about 'an unsightly timber shed and sawpit', but John sharply pointed out that shipwrights were necessary to a port. Fleetwood was beginning to boom so why complain?

What an exciting time it must have been when ships of all shapes and sizes were being built on the Wyre! Barquetines, brigantines, etc, were arriving on every tide. The year of 1862 saw the launch of the 107-ton schooner *Richard Warbrick* whose figurehead was carved by a Workington man in the likeness of Mr Warbrick's son. Shingle on the slipway delayed the launch of the magnificent oak vessel but this was achieved at the next high tide by Miss Agnes Warbrick armed with a bottle of champagne.

The following year the windows of Queen's Terrace were crammed with people watching John's second smooth launching, that of the schooner *Sarah Ann Dickenson*. Mrs Whiteside of the Fleetwood Arms laid on a sumptuous dinner at which John spoke in praise of the schooner's rigger, Mr Coulborn: 'He has brought out the beauty and sailing capacity of the vessel and has had as much to do with the final cut as the tailor has to do with the making of the man.' It was the launching of the schooner *Agnes* that attracted the greatest ever number of spectators to Fleetwood.

By 1867 John Gibson was fighting the Gas Company on behalf of Fleetwood residents. Not only did the gas smell awful, it was too highly priced. Furthermore, how dare the Company close Cop Lane, a public right of way? He fought also to protect the Mount, which was constantly threatened by encroaching seas. It was he who urged the Commissioners and Sir Peter Hesketh Fleetwood to do something.

Fleetwood in the 1900s. Mr Porter's Fleet, cargo ships of the Wyre Shipping Co., with a host of spectators on the esplanade. (Author's collection)

By 1868 the 158-ton schooner *Ellen Widdup* was on the stocks, following in a blaze of glory by schooners *Useful*, *Elizabeth and Ann*, *Agnes* and the two-masted ketches *William and John*, and *Ezra*. On 26 February 1869 *Sarah Ann Widdup*, another schooner for Warbrick's, was launched, but it was 1870 that in retrospect proved a sad year. The fine, three-masted schooner *Manchester* with the steam tug *Jabez Bunting* in attendance had been launched without a hitch. At the Crown Hotel dinner the toast was to 'the lovely child of hoary old man Manchester and fair nymph Fleetwood'. Just fifteen months later the ill-fated *Manchester*, on a voyage from Stockholm to Barrow with a cargo of steel, disappeared without trace. All the crew were lost.

The pinnacle of John's career was marked by the barquentine *Emily Warbrick*, the sixteenth vessel from Gibson's yard. Launched in March 1872 after eighteen months in construction, she was the largest ever built in the town, 104ft in length and 23ft 4ins in beam. The population turned out in force. The band of the forty-seventh Regiment from Euston Barracks filled the salty air with stirring music and at 1p.m., as the tide reached 20ft, the daggers were knocked from under her keel and off she glided to the tune of 'Britannia Rules the Waves'. This time shareholders and friends proceeded to the Royal Hotel where the beautifully scrolled menu showed forty items from which to choose. The pride of the whole town was expressed in the *Emily Warbrick*, 'a vessel as beautiful as the young lady whose name she bears.' That young lady was to marry the schooner's commander, Captain Poole.

John went on to buy the Bonded Warehouses in Dock Street but industrial action set trade back when a number of his workmen left to earn higher wages at the shipyard in Strand Road, Preston. Although trade recovered, with the launching of the schooner *Esther* in 1875, John, who died in 1877, never saw the opening of the long-awaited Dock at Fleetwood, but his sons played a big part in the festivities. The chandlery shop at the bonded warehouse was decorated with flags and golden eagles. Gibson's block shop opposite the stone quay where schooners were fitted out after launching was similarly resplendent.

The last of the large schooners built on Gibson's riverside site, the *John Gibson*, christened by Miss M.A. Porter, daughter of Edmund Porter, glided down the ways in 1878. In June 1890 Gibson's suffered a great blow. Their extensive premises, situated only 40 yards from two gas holders, caught fire, causing a crowd of inhabitants to flee in terror to the shelter of the Mount. Fortunately the wind fanned the flames away from the gasworks. The Town Fire Brigade and Military Fire Brigade battled nobly but had to abandon all hope of saving Gibson's mainly wooden premises in order to safeguard surrounding property. It was 8a.m. the following day before the fire was put out.

The firm never really recovered and the family never forgave the Railway Company who had shown no sympathy for shipbuilding and twice displaced the firm. However, under James Gibson, the business, famous for its high standard of workmanship, carried on. The yard now concentrated on small craft: half-deck boats; pleasure steamers;

prawners; fishing smacks; ferry boats. Wealthy yachtsmen from Barrow to Bangor and beyond aspired to owning a Gibson-built racing yacht, especially when the renowned designer William Stoba was involved. He it was who designed the legendary yacht *Zulu*, but that is another story.

In 1902 Gibson's shipbuilding business changed hands, purchased by Liver and Wilding. George Gibson, born 1851, son of James lived until he was eighty-five. A freemason, he started his career in Drewry's shop, the grocers which supplied Queen Victoria's yacht with freshly ground coffee on her visit to Fleetwood. George, who quickly owned his own business, was an exponent of Tonic Solfa singing. Four of the family sang in the choir at the Congregational Church. This was indeed a family that made a great contribution to the town. Without them, the exciting days of sail would not have been half as exciting.

Richard Warbrick, a famous top sail schooner built on the beach at Fleetwood, 'dressed overall' for launching. (Author's collection)

CHAPTER 15

'WHAT MEAN THESE STONES?'

—✶—

In the early hours of a cold winter's morning, two distinguished Fleetwood firms (sadly no more) set about the formidable task of moving a carved 4-ton stone. This was no ordinary stone. It had been given kindly by the British Transport Docks Board to the Fleetwood Civic Society and there was a mystery about its origin. What was no mystery was the fact that this giant object was intrinsic to the town of Fleetwood, sure to be of great interest to local and railway historians alike. Thus the stone was worthy to be moved from its ignominious site behind the docks; a site where once stood Fleetwood's very first railway station which was little more than a wooden hut when the first train chugged over the timber trestle on 15 July 1840. That exciting opening day for the Preston and Wyre Railway deserved better. For years, Sir Peter Hesketh Fleetwood had striven in sickness and in health. He had given money until he was nearly bankrupt in order to build the line. Sadly, the grand station that replaced the first humble one is also no more, but to return to the stone, what was the history behind it? What was the mystery? For years it had lain amidst weeds and thistles in an abandoned area, shared by derelict inshore boats and rusting steam trawlers, fit only for scrap.

The question of a Dock for Fleetwood had been continuously in mind since 1837. Indeed in the 1860s it was stated that £16,000 was being lost annually for the want of this facility. Spurred on, the Lancashire and Yorkshire Railway Company purchased 600 acres of the Fleetwood Estate lying between the 1840 and 1851 embankments for £25,000. Construction commenced, the Docks had walls 40ft high of Longridge stone and Cornish granite. Foundations were 30ft deep, and the entrance lock measured 250ft long by 50ft wide, its wrought-iron gates weighing 60 tons. The total area covered 67 acres with 8 miles of railway track and a timber pond. 8 October 1877 witnessed a Grand Procession in Fleetwood. The Chairman of the Railway Company T. Barnes announced 'I name this Wyre Dock and declare it open to the commerce of the world'.

'What mean these stones?' – Lancashire and Yorkshire Railway. (Author's collection)

The Procession was over a mile long. A medal depicting a three-masted barque and a locomotive was struck and distributed.

The length of Dock Street was like a fair. Stands for the sale of gingerbreads, nuts, sweets and fruit were set up and 'Aunt Sally shooting galleries, weighing machines, mechanical figures, galvanic batteries and itinerant musicians and singers'. Craft on the river were gaily decorated with flags, from the humblest to the stately *Duke of Connaught*. The *Fleetwood Chronicle* reported and from all accounts everyone had a jolly good time. Imports of grain immediately increased and the Lancashire and Yorkshire Railway erected a huge grain elevator on the east side of the Dock, ready for use in 1883, it was what we now call 'State of the Art'. As time went on, the grand Elevator with its 'Jumbo' (Canadian style) proved not the success hoped for. Trawler and inshore fishing took over from timber and cargo trade. The Elevator, now more a White Elephant than a Jumbo, was dismantled in 1939, it being such a target from the air for German enemy aircraft it had to go. Was the huge stone in question from the base of the Elevator? Or, was it as some people think a stone brought by sea for a new, grand hoped-for Fleetwood Railway Station, which like the Dock was so long in coming, that the commemorative stone lay forgotten and neglected for years? Carved by the Stocks Brothers it may be one of the earliest railway commemorative stones still in existence. Why was it delivered to the old site on the Docks? And why did it lie sinking there, unwept, unhonoured and unsung? The indications are that it dates from the 1870s when Fleetwood was booming. Study the carvings and you will wonder why it was from inception not given a place of honour. It shows a train leaving a tunnel, a steam packet paddle steamer and the Legs of Man.

Fleetwood had a connection with the Isle of Man going back to before 1830. It could have been built into the Grain Elevator and left forlorn when the rest of the remains were carted away. High up in the Canadian-style elevator its date was displayed in white tiles visible, some said, from Bleasdale Fells. Brown and Jackson of Copse Road and James Robertson and Sons Ltd of Wyre Dock conveyed the massive moment to Euston Park and on 1 May 1976 it was handed over to the townspeople of Fleetwood in the presence of the late Walter Clegg MP and the late William Brown, deputy lieutenant of Lancashire. A poignant piece of Fleetwood's history was, at last, in a more honoured resting place.

CHAPTER 16

GLASSON DOCK

—⚙—

Historian Edward Baines reported a spacious dock built at Glasson in 1787 when it was a village on the River Lune near Thurnham. This dock could receive twenty-five large merchant vessels whose cargoes were forwarded by lighters to Lancaster port which was silting.

Conder Green looking towards the snow-capped Bleasdale Fells in February 2010. A tiny settlement not far from Glasson. Two massive cannons from the Crimean War used to grace the entrance to Conder Green's Stork Inn. (Author's collection)

Glasson Dock, near Lancaster, 2010. (Author's collection)

The Victoria Inn at Glasson Dock, 2010. (Author's collection)

Glasson Dock, area given over as a marina, note the lock gates. March 2010. (Author's collection)

Glasson Dock, March 2010. (Author's collection)

Shipyard workers were accommodated in cottages known as the 'Ten Row', built at the same time as the Lancaster Port Commissioners ordered the wet dock. The City of Liverpool ship called regularly.

There was a coastal hamlet called Glasson long before Glasson Dock was built. In the 1930s the lock gates linked two dock basins with massive stone sides. Although it never became the busy shipping centre visualised by Lancaster merchants, it was still a port worthwhile for certain trades – shipbuilding and repair was the work of Nicholson and Sons (established 1840), rigging, handling buoys, winches, ventilators, hatch covers and so on in their growing dock. By the early 1850s, although able to cope with ocean-going craft, weekenders and sailors 'messing about in boats' were looking to it as a marina.

Glasson is a port along the western coast that has revived after flagging fortunes. Although the original West Indies trade died, Glasson has become an important boating centre and its coastal trade is being well-handled by its dock, once again.

Glasson Dock, March 2010. (Author's collection)

CHAPTER 17

SOUTHPORT AND FORMBY

Early fishermen of Southport were often fishermen by day but willing also to serve on the first official lifeboat *Jessie Knowles*, payment by day being 10s, or 20s for service at night. The Southport coxswain, William Rockcliffe, in the first lifeboat rescue, brought 212 people safely to shore. Generations of the Parkinson family were all lifeboatmen.

One of the fiercest storms in the Irish Sea, 1897. An artist's impression of the Southport Lifeboat. (Author's collection)

Pleasure boat *Emperor*, arriving from the south of England on a visit to Southport, 2 August 1928. (Author's collection)

Southport, Pier and Marine Lake. (Author's collection)

Left: Formby Lifeboat *Jessie Knowles.* (Author's collection)

Below: Unknown wreck off Formby, 1898. It probably sailed from Liverpool. (Author's collection)

Out fishing, they collected oysters and shrimps to sell to visitors and to supply Broadbents Oyster Bar in Coronation Street, Southport. Oysters and ale were popular with the seaside visitors. There was Mrs Moor's shop in Nevill Street with its large board 'Mrs Moor's potted meat'.

Potted shrimps and beef were sold to visitors and residents. Famous customers included Lord Derby and Martin Harvey, the famous actor. Her potted shrimps were famous but Mrs Moor also sold treacle toffee, lemon pickle, jams and marmalade.

The sands at Southport were busy even in the 1840s the time of the port's first fishing fleet. Even then there was a 'bathing season' when carriages left every day from the Hesketh Arms, the Union Hotel and Clare's Livery Stables to meet the boats from Manchester and Liverpool to convey passengers to Southport.

The coach 'Eclipse' left every morning for Liverpool at 8a.m. and returned at 7p.m. There was also a coach to Bolton. Thomas Rimmer was the main carrier then for Southport and he went to Liverpool every Tuesday and Friday. Even before Southport was thought of, crowds of people went to what became the Churchdown area on 'big Bathing Sunday'. They came to this fair in carts from Crossens, Banks, Hawes Side and Birkdale. William Sutton on his way to Scotland observed this and decided to put up a bathing house at South Hawes, built from wreck timbers. As creator of what was called 'Duke's Folly', he became known as the 'Red Duke'. Vessels could at that time anchor in the bay which was then 11 fathoms deep. William Sutton was buried on 29 May 1840, his original 'Folly' becoming the Royal Hotel. A lane led through the sandhills to 'Little London'. The Ash Tree or 'Isle of Wight' inn at Birkdale was where well-known 'Fiddler Harry' played for dancing parties. In the vicinity of North Meols there was a fine bay 17 fathoms deep, but it became choked with sand so that vessels could no longer ride at anchor.

Formby Lifeboatman John Alndow, 1890s. (Author's collection)

Water colour sketch, possibly by David Cox (1783 – 1859) off the Lancashire coast. (Author's collection)

CHAPTER 18

LANCASTER

—◦◦◦—

Lancaster in the middle of the eighteenth century was second only to London as a port shipping cargoes to the West Indies. The Romans built a fort overlooking the River Lune, remnants of which unfortunately were to cause an impediment to shipping. The centre of the old port was based on St George's Quay with the old Customs House nearby but the port died because of silting up, although the use of the Lancaster Canal was an effort to keep trade going northwards to Kendal and southwards to Glasson Dock. Amongst the many important merchants in Lancaster's heyday was Augustine Greenwood who wrote: 'the master of a vessel owned and freighted in partnership was an important personage in those early days since on his skill no less in buying and selling, as in seamanship depended the success of the voyage.'

Research brings interesting pieces of history to light. On 22 January 1820, a fine ship called the *Helen Jane* intended for the East India trade was launched by Messrs Finlay, Wilson and Company. At 562 tons …'it is one of the largest, private ships that has been built for trade from this port'. It was for Mr Gladstone, the statesman, and coincided with a heavy fall of snow on that day which caused the London Mail Coach to be twenty-two hours late on arrival in Lancaster. Candles were sent to the West Indies and Mr Gillow exported 'great quantities of mahogany furniture … his extensive ware-rooms are stored with every article of useful and ornamental mahogany furniture'.

And what of Lancaster in the new millennium? Fine furniture production, made famous by Waring and Gillow ended in 1962. The University at Bailrigg was founded in 1964 and Lancaster's Customs House made into a Marine Museum in 1985. Silting of the port continues and Heysham now handles shipping further facilitated by Glasson Dock.

The King's Arms, Kendal, in the 1880s. Kendal was once a town with strong trade links to the port of Lancaster via the River Kent. (Author's collection)

Opposite above: John of Gaunt's Tower, Lancaster – the county town of Lancashire and once a port greater than Liverpool. (Author's collection)

Opposite below: River Kent – important for trade with Kendal town. (Author's collection)

CHAPTER 19

MORECAMBE AND MORECAMBE BAY

Until cheap rail excursions caused expansion and changed its name to Morecambe, Poulton-le-Sands was a small village. There was a harbour and jetty for the fishing fleet and a second jetty in 1855 when passenger and cargo trade developed, foreshadowing the deep-water port at Heysham which opened fifty years later. At the time of an 1897 photograph showing Morecambe's promenade and pier the fleet consisted of 120 prawners operated by Morecambe Trawlers Association, which set prices for fish, cockles and mussels. About 200 sailing and rowing boats catered for holiday makers, regattas being a feature as early as 1836 when on 14 July. Mr Bower in Nimrod 'won the sailing match for two silver goblets'. Prior to the Regatta Dinner the Gold Cup Members' Plate and £50 Maiden Plate were competed for. A horse-drawn coach, Old Times, used to clatter out from Lancaster to Old Poulton Hall, now demolished, but once owned by the Washingtons of Warton. At the end of Central Pier was moored the fleet of nobbies. Heavy horses and strong carts were an alternative means of collecting the famous Morecambe Bay prawns by dragging huge nets amongst the shallows. With boiler on board and still using an 18ft beam trawl and riddle, Andy Jarvis' *Linda* is one of the last remaining nobbies. The departure of fishing boats from Fleetwood into the occasionally treacherous Morecambe Bay could once prove disastrous, when a fair wind could change rapidly to a squall, tearing freshly barked sails to ribbons. In December 1834 a subscription was set up for 'the poor fishermen who had lost their boats, nets and stakes in the late storm at Poulton-le-Sands.' In a heavy gale only four years later all the fishing boats at Morecambe were driven from their moorings.

Thomas Ward had a ship-breaking yard at Morecambe to which ocean-going liners like *Tchad* were towed. In thick mist fishermen found the bang of heavy hammers a useful guide home. The sailing trawlers of Morecambe Bay were considered to have finer underwater lines, which made for greater speed than those registered at other ports such as Brixham. In this connection William Stoba, ship's architect for Armours, was well known beyond the Bay for his designs. Fishing families like the Baxters, Rimmers, Sumners and Wrights revelled in 'winning the pennant', a flag depicting a fighting cock, 2ft at the mast, 6ft to tail. Whichever smack arrived first at the fishing grounds was winner and could fly the pennant. By a stroke of luck, such as wind change, a slow vessel could win, but favourites were *Surprise II*, *Louie Rigby*, *Reliance*, *Margaret* and *Harriet*. In 1915 Margaret brought in the crew of a coal ship sunk by a German submarine, *U-21*, off the Bar Light Vessel, Liverpool. The great bay of Morecambe, subject to violent storms and vast accumulations of sand, nevertheless benefits from the scouring action of tides passing up and down the rivers. Without this, estuaries and harbour mouths would be hopelessly overcome by silt.

Above: Mona's Queen, Fleetwood, Isle of Man vessel paddle-steamer. (Author's collection)

Above: Aboard a steam trawler in Morecambe Bay, 1915. (Author's collection)

Below: Devil's Bridge, in the near distance, at Kirkby Lonsdale spans the River Lune, famous for fishing, part of the way along its journey to Morecambe Bay, 1944. (Author's collection)

Left: Morecambe Bay frozen in 1895. (Author's collection)

Below: A group of lifeboatmen in 1920, including Dick Abrams, 'Chuck' Wilson, Peter Wright, Tom and Jack Leadbetter outside the old lifeboat house in Fleetwood. Most were fishermen who knew Morecambe Bay well. (Author's collection)

Morecambe, in the very early days, consisted of a stone jetty and three small fishing boats but the spectacular view across Morecambe Bay to the mountains of the Lake District caused the entrepreneurs to single its future out as a popular seaside resort. As the 'donkeys on the sands, Morecambe' picture postcard proves (see page 115) – big ships and pleasure steamers could also make an appearance in 1908.

In 1876 the loss of a well-known herring boat was reported. Two Morecambe fishermen left Morecambe in the herring-boat *Leader* bound for Silloth. Caught in a squall the boat foundered 2 miles from Morecambe Lightship. A search found the *Leader*'s mast visible at low water. John Edmondson, father of eight children and Adam Raby, twenty-one years old and unmarried were presumed drowned.

MORECAMBE BAY

The *Maude Pickup* lifeboat had the most distinguished record off the Fylde coast –
between 1894 and 1930, 117 lives were saved. On 16 June 1897 the *Maude Pickup*
made history by rescuing eighteen men from three wrecks. The crew were: Tom Perry,
Nicholas Abram, 'Judy' Wright, David Leadbetter, Toby Wright, Jack Leadbetter (cox),
Dick Leadbetter (Second cox), Jim Roskell, John Salthouse, Charlie Hughes, Matt
Boardman, F. Bettes, Matt Cowell and Lawrence Bond.

Steam trawler *Doris* FD 141 in Lune Deeps. Pilot Boat, *Leader* or *Falcon* (centre). (Author's collection)

The village of Bare near Heysham Port in 1900. (Author's collection)

Left: William Leadbetter, lifeboat man and sailor, pictured in Morecambe Bay. (Author's collection)

Below: Two faces of Morecambe – shipping and pleasure. (Author's collection)

DONKEYS ON THE SANDS, MORECAMBE.   Nº 464.

CHAPTER 20

I AM SAILING – THE MANX CONNECTION

—◦◦◦—

In 1842 a service was opened from Fleetwood to Mona's Isle, now commonly known as the Isle of Man. The fare was 4s, 6s first class. Indeed, the Mona's Isle Company existed as early as 1829. During those years a strong tradition of service and friendship steadily built up between Fleetwood and the Island. Thousands of passengers were carried in fair weather and foul.

Individual boats were famous, one of which, TSS *Manxman*, was to become the only remaining passenger steam ferry in Britain. Her sister ship, *Mona's Isle*, was scrapped in 1980 and there was speculation in the world of shipping that *Manxman* would follow her to the breaker's yard. Although capable of carrying 2,303 passengers, on her last sailing from Fleetwood there were only 490 on board, the revenue from which was not enough to pay for the bunker oil to fire her turbines. Saved by a group of businessmen and enthusiasts, she was eventually berthed at Preston Dock and billed as 'Europe's last remaining steam-powered passenger liner', she became a Day Visitor Centre and Museum and was also used in film sets, notably *The Missionary*, *Chariots of Fire* and *SoS Titanic*. It is with much affection that I recall going aboard to meet Judith Roberts of Radio Lancashire when my book *Shipwrecks of the North West* was launched. Built by Cammell Laird of Birkenhead at a cost of £847,000, she was launched on 8 February 1955. Of 2,495 gross tonnage, with a speed of 20 knots, in her heyday *Manxman* had a crew of sixty-eight.

This noteworthy steamer whose excellence had contributed towards many enjoyable holidays in the Isle of Man calls to mind another conspicuous vessel amongst a great line – the *Viking* – built in 1905, the first turbine steamer owned by the Manx Company. On 25 May 1907, *Viking* made her fastest crossing from Fleetwood, Lune Buoy to Douglas Head in two hours twenty-two minutes, achieving an average speed of 23.2 knots, Season after season, like an old friend, thousands witnessed her departures and arrivals, so that when at last she was withdrawn in August 1954, appropriately her bell was presented to the town of Fleetwood. An inscribed mounting made from her timbers placed below the bell gave details of her distinguished career including war service, but was wrongly inscribed 'Average speed 33.2 knots'. For some time the magnificent bell in silent indignation pronounced this a real clanger, but happily the newly designed Viking Bar in the Marine Hall, one of the many attractions of 1982 Maritime Heritage Year, put the record straight.

Another final slipping of moorings and sinking of hearts came about on 12 September 1965. It was 'Goodbye Ben' when *Ben My Chree* sailed at midnight from Douglas to Liverpool with the last of the Grand Prix visitors. After forty years' service to the Island the oldest and best-loved of the Manx Steamers was sold. She was the first crack ship to have one funnel and many new navigational aids such as searchlight, fog signals and a depth sounder that could be used even when the ship was going at full speed. My father, without hesitation always cited *Ben My Chree* as his favourite ship, a view shared by Merseyside shipspotters interviewed at the time on BBC *Look North*. She did 200 trips a season and carried millions of passengers from the Irish Sea ports to the Isle of Man. The *Ben*'s first passage, made on 29 June 1927, was historically interesting as it coincided with the day after a total eclipse of the sun, which her many passengers had travelled north to witness. Memories linger of beautiful wood panelling, the gold and white ceiling of the first-class lounge, glorious rose and lavender decor and her slim, white hull. On her last trip she was commanded by the Commodore, Captain W. Cain, reputed during his twenty-two years in charge to have carried more passengers than any slipmaster in the Company. The last weekend of *Ben*'s career was marked by a gathering of the World Ship Society. A later *Ben My Chree* played an historic part on 1 July 1979, the year of the Manx Millennium. The Viking longship *Odin's Raven*, specially designed and built for the occasion, was sailing from Norway to the Island. On passage from Ardrossan to Douglas, in an unscheduled stop off Port Patrick, Captain Jack E. Ronan brought the *Ben My Chree* alongside the longship to enable passengers to take photographs. He was presented with a photograph of *Odin's Raven*, signed by all members of its crew, a uniquely historic occasion. Slipped moorings of another kind, unintentional, occurred on the wild and stormy night in January 1976 when the *King Orry* broke away in Glasson Dock and wandered onto Cockerham Marshes, but that is another story in the history of the great Manx ships: Perhaps – 'Look, no hands!'

Talking of storms, the equally famous Belfast boats whose long, proud Fleetwood service closed on 28 April 1928, also faced calm and tempest in their thousands of crossings of the Irish Sea. In late December 1894 Captain John Cook, a tough, courageous Scottish sea veteran on the Fleetwood to Belfast run, had the unenviable task of battling against a cyclone. At 120mph it struck the north-west coast of Lancashire, breaking amongst other things the Meteorological Society's wind recording instrument on the Mount at Fleetwood. Anxious crowds gathered near the railway station, straining their eyes towards the horizon, fervently hoping for the safe arrival of the *Duke of York* with 400 passengers all longing to get home for Christmas. Leaving Belfast at 8a.m., aware of the imminent gale, Captain Cook soon considered making for the Ballama lightship. In worsening weather the starboard engine stopped but fortunately the engineer

Left: 'We are sailing' – Catherine and Eddie Rothwell pictured in 1970, during the days of their early retirement, off to the Isle of Man from Fleetwood on *Manxman* or *Tynwald*. (Author's collection)

Below: Port St Mary, 1895, Isle of Man. The Isle of Man's Steam packet vessels steamed millions of miles but had a number of mishaps, for example, *Peel Castle* ran aground 7 June 1924. *Fenella* finally towed her clear of sandbanks off Douglas. (Author's collection)

managed to get it going, so with plenty of coal available they tried for Fleetwood. The ship battled on towards Walney, by which time coal was running low. Discounting the Morecambe Bay Lightship because of its uncertainty, Captain Cook resolved to make one last attempt and with all in readiness for emergency he ran for the only landmark, Wyre light, just managing to clear the bank and gain the comparative safety of the Channel. At long last, at precisely 4p.m., amidst cheers they made landfall with ninety terrified female passengers, several injured crew and everything moveable having been washed overboard. It was the worst cyclone that either Chief Mate Higham or Captain Cook ever remembered. In fact they learned later that its shock had killed Christopher Smith, Captain of the Morecambe Bay Lightship. Forty letters of gratitude were sent to Captain Cook from passengers thankful for their safe deliverance. The Directors of the Lancashire and Yorkshire Railway Company and North Western Railway Company granted an extra week's wage to the crew.

The old Port at Piel, Isle of Man. (Author's collection)

The historic cyclone in the Irish Sea was a compulsive topic of conversation over Christmas dinner that year. Captain John Cook was not forgotten. As Master of the *Thomas Dugdale*, a position he held for thirty-four years, he crossed the Irish Sea 8,000 times, becoming Commodore in 1875, Upon retiring, he lived in Fleetwood and saw the final Irish sailing in 1928. Two years later he died at the age of eighty-three. The words of Gavin Sutherland's hit song of the 1980s seem to be particularly appropriate to Fleetwood: 'I am sailing ....stormy waters. I am flying like a bird across the sea.'

The SS *Douglas* sailed from the Isle of Man in the 1860s, clearly visible from the Bispham cliffs. This early paddle steamer was built in 1858 although the Isle of Man Steam Co. had used a sloop of the same name under Captain Quayle in the 1830s. Trade to and from the island had increased greatly. The company figurehead for SS *Tynwald* in 1845 proudly showed a full-length Manx Scandinavian King in armour to emphasise they had arrived and were proud of their Scandinavian origins.

Rushen Castle, Isle of Man. (Author's collection)

Above left: Laxey Wheel, summer 1995, Isle of Man (Author's collection)

Above right: Port Erin, Isle of Man. (Author's collection)

CHAPTER 21

ST ANNES ON SEA AND HUNTCLIFF

Although you would never associate St Annes (now coupled to Lytham) with ports, once its pier opened on 15 June it was a calling place with a landing jetty for pleasure boats, in particular the *Wellington*. Summer sailings went on to Morecambe. Like so many others this popular pier suffered from fire. Following a disastrous fire in 1972, the Floral Hall was destroyed by fire in 1982. 1 May 1927 had been a triumph when the town was granted a Charter and the townspeople celebrated this Charter Day with a gathering of lifeboats and a procession.

The new town in the sand hills was by then very different. It became a popular seaside resort and the days when the first post office was opened at Alpha House, Clement Rawstron being the first postman and the Heap family, pioneers, lived at Pine Cottage, the first rated house, were remembered by but a few. Handloom weaving was gone along with turf dales when every tenant had right to dig turf from the mossland for his kitchen fireplace, part of all thatched cottages. The blacksmith's forge was across from the Trawl Boat Inn but this hostelry became so rowdy it too had to go. In St Annes is a memorial to the worst lifeboat disaster in British history. In 1886 the St Annes lifeboat went to the rescue of the German barque *Mexico*, and the thirteen-man crew of the lifeboat were all drowned.

Southport lifeboat had also set off to answer *Mexico*'s distress calls and fourteen of their lifeboat crew were drowned, just two men surviving. The third lifeboat that answered was, with great difficulty, able to help the sinking ship *Mexico* but this terrible tragedy will never be forgotten on the Fylde Coast. Funds poured in from many parts of the world including Germany and lifeboat design was improved.

As for Pine Cottage, when the railway came, part of the track ran alongside, so having built a large fine house in St Annes, Wilson Heap found it most convenient to pass his furniture over the boundary fence and have it loaded into waiting railway trucks ready to chug along to his new home in fashionable St Annes.

Of all the ships that have foundered on the coast of Lancashire in memorable storms one of the luckiest 'landings' was that of the *Huntcliff* in February 1894. Such was the wind force and flood of seas inland, that rabbits and hares were seen running down the streets in Lytham, driven from their sandhills home. Large advertising boards were uprooted and carried away, lead was ripped from roofs, but all such incidents paled into insignificance compared with the stranding of the steamship *Huntcliff* on the twelfth.

She was a cargo boat for which George Horsley & Sons of Hartlepool had paid £36,000 only two years before; an 'ocean tramp', 350ft in length with a registered tonnage of 2,018 and engines equivalent to 1,700 horse power. Alongside her, the *Sirene*, stranded in October 1892, would have looked comparatively paltry. The crew consisted of twenty-seven men, the Wilkes brothers of Middlesborough being in charge of the magnificent engines. Five Arabs and a Zulu looked after the stoking department and unbeknown to the captain, there were two stowaways on board.

Having made the run from Java to New York with sugar, *Huntcliff* had come to Liverpool with a cargo of cotton from Charlestown. Bound for Cardiff, where she planned to load coals at Barry Dock for Aden, she left Liverpool at 2p.m. on Sunday carrying only water ballast and with a pilot on board. Absence of a cargo meant that a tremendous amount of hull was exposed to the violence of wind and waves, when at 5p.m., just about 4 miles off Great Orme's Head, gales began.

Despite her weight and size, the vessel was swung round with ease for the rudder had no hold of the water and when sails were set to keep her 'head-on', the canvas was torn from the rigging like paper. Efforts to fix tarpaulins in the mizzen rigging were also futile. It was later said: 'If we had only had half a cargo we should have been able to steam against it'.

Captain Howell and Chief Officer Peterson decided to lie as near as possible to the coast of Llandudno, and so dropped anchor. But their plan failed. Worse still, the anchor could not be hauled up again and 120 fathoms of chain had finally to be sacrificed to the angry sea.

With the power of steam subdued, they could neither shelter nor put back into Liverpool. Broadside on, in the teeth of the gale, *Huntcliff* rolled so fearfully, at the mercy of wind and ocean, that the crew had a hard time holding on. Their hands were sore with the effort. Terrified, the Arabs moved hither and thither about the companionways, and the stowaways, who had thought only of a cheap passage to Cardiff, dearly wished they had never come.

Between 5p.m. on Sunday afternoon and 2a.m. on Monday morning, the *Huntcliff* was blown at the caprice of the elements until she bumped at St Annes. No stationary lights were seen during that appalling night. And so the hours dragged on, with the crew having no idea where they were, until the vessel was finally deposited, quite undamaged, on the sandy bottom of the beach not far from the convalescent home and only 50 yards from the sandhills. A better place for beaching could not have been chosen. Not one of her steel plates was buckled and there was many a joke made afterwards to the effect that: '*Huntcliff* is her name and she lived up to it.'

News of the stranding of such a magnificent boat travelled fast. Crowds poured in from all over the district. Professional photographers, known in the nineteenth century as 'the professors of the dark art', swarmed alongside amateurs. At high tide clouds of spray broke over the decks and spectators venturing near received a thorough soaking.

Ice-cream stalls and fruit sellers set up; by Wednesday the area of the vessel was described as a veritable fairground. 800 people visited the scene, many brought in by railway, and so great was the crowd that few were allowed on board. Someone offered the chief mate twopence to show him round. 'I'll give you sixpence to clear off', was the swift reply, and the general opinion of the crew seemed to be that St Annes was a 'one horse place.' No doubt there were souvenir hunters galore. Someone set up a collecting box for the convalescent home opposite the stranded steamer. Meanwhile, discussions went on as how to move *Huntcliff*. The underwriters sent Mr W. Horsley and Captain Young of Liverpool to size up the situation. As she was insured for £35,000, they were determined to float the *Huntcliff* at any cost. Should a channel be dug for her passage to the sea? The steam tug-boat *Ranger* was expected to arrive with stores on board for this operation. Another plan was to build a slip under her, lifting the tremendous weight by hydraulic jacks and to refloat on the 28ft tide expected on 20 February. This first method had already worked in the 1860s for a schooner which came ashore below the central pier of Blackpool.

On 24 May, they managed it. Meanwhile, the Arabs had been embroiled in a knife fight ashore and another member of the crew had been found incapable on the genteel pavement of St Annes 'with a bottle of whiskey for a pillow'. So it was that both ships' crew and townspeople breathed a sigh of relief as *Huntcliff* turned towards Liverpool, home and beauty.

CHAPTER 22

OVERTON AND SUNDERLAND POINT

—◦◦◦—

As an ancient calling place for ships Overton, typified by its church belfry for the parish church of St Helen, is considered to be the oldest in Lancashire. W. James Thompson of Barrow presented the bell in January 1878 but the Anglo-Norman doorway, just out of sight with its beaked and chevron ornament, has been dated between 1050 and 1140. The Woodhouse family built boats for 300 years, commencing in 1660. Cockersand Abbey stone is said to have gone in to some Overton houses which were supplied with spinning wheels for the American cotton landed at nearby Sunderland Point. Here, as at Glasson, 'haaf', draught and drift net fishing has been carried on for centuries; also 'whammeling' which uses a 300 yard drift net. The haaf or lave net is a net bag attached to an 18ft long pole supported by three legs. The Gardner family who still whammel in old, lugsail-rigged boats were also well-known River Lune pilots. James Spencer of Sunderland Point piloted vessels for five shillings a journey. Including his son's service. this family did the job for ninety years. Francis Raby, an Overton man, was the first keeper of Abbey Scar Lighthouse, Cockersand and of Plover Scar Lighthouse, another job that stayed in one family for generations. He was paid £25 a year but augmented this by making baskets for mussel gatherers. Snatchem's Marsh, 2 miles of tidal road, cuts off Sunderland Point twice daily, but it was the port for Lancaster with an extensive West Indies and African trade. Gunpowder-carrying vessels tied up by the Powder Stump, considered a safer distance. Once the fourth port for the West Indies trade, Glasson with its safer anchorage replaced Sunderland whose best known inhabitant was perhaps the little black boy Sambo. It is more likely that he died of cholera than of grief when one reads of 'alarming accounts of the progress of cholera at Sunderland.' But Sambo was not entirely alone in an alien land. Parish registers show that Alice Singleton of Norbreck near Blackpool married a negro servant Samuel Hutchinson in 1750.

Because of more fears of cholera, it was especially ordered that a fast day was to be observed 'with marked solemnity', as demonstrated by Queen Victoria herself on other occasions, because of the deaths that had occurred. Churches were so crowded that people stood in the aisles. There was a meeting to decide how expenses could be defrayed for guarding against the cholera. Money came from the Poor rate for the lime washing of vehicles. By August 1843 a Sunderland Point regatta was held, cholera forgotten.

A famous pilot there was John Gerrard who died at Sunderland aged 102. Newspapers reported that less than a year before his death he rowed a boat across the River Lune. Further news in the *Lancaster Gazette* on 15 November 1834 tells of Captain James Charnley of the ship *Thetis* who, on a voyage to Barbados beat off the French privateer *Bonaparte* and the inhabitants of Dominica presented him with silver plate plus £240 to be divided amongst his crew. *Thetis* carried eighteen 6-pounder guns and a crew of forty-five whilst *Bonaparte* had a crew of 215 and carried twenty 9-pounder guns. Robert Lawson made Sunderland Point a busy centre of trade in timber and cotton. Edward Baines said of Sunderland that cotton wool was brought there before it came to Liverpool, but its use was not understood: 'People came for miles to inspect it as a curiosity and it lay in Robert Lawson's warehouse more than a year before a purchaser could be found.' When the Jacobites marched on Lancaster in 1715 they seized six cannons from one of Lawson's ships anchored off the Point.

On the right bank of the River Lune after flowing through marshes and passing Glasson Dock port, there still remain parts of a port at Sunderland Point. There was once a prosperous harbour in what now seems an unlikely situation, because a Quaker

Sunderland Hall where Robert Lawson lived. (Author's collection)

Sunderland Point, 2010. (Author's collection)

merchant, Robert Lawson developed it as a port for Lancaster. In the seventeenth century there was an anchorage with a quay and warehouses. Cotton supplies arrived here from the West Indies with rum and tobacco. A kapok or cotton tree still grows in the village but more interesting is Sambo's grave, honouring a faithful black slave. It is said Sambo died of a broken heart for his master never returned to bring him back to the West Indies, probably because trade died at Sunderland Point with the failure of Robert Lawson's wealth. Sambo is still remembered, however, in the epitaph on his grave, part of which reads: 'Full many a sand bird chirps upon the sod and many an elfin round him trips. Full many a sunbeam warms the clod and many a teeming cloud upon him drips.'

This doggerel epitaph also states that 'Sambo, the faithful Negro died' on arrival at Sunderland Point, which may well be the stark truth. An old building, thought to be a bath house for sailors, is further evidence of an old and now vanished port.

Nowadays to reach the village which has one of the smallest houses in Lancashire the motorist must take the Morecambe Road and turn left at Overton always bearing in mind that Sunderland Point is cut off by road from the rest of Lancashire whenever the tide comes in.

CHAPTER 23

ARNSIDE AND SANDSIDE

—◆◆◆—

Vessels travelling coastwise were usefully alerted by systems of lights, landmarks and buoys. Once guided into port, it was a duty to call at the Customs House, although sometimes men from the Water Guard would board a vessel on its way in. The 1978 photograph shows the customs house at Arnside, now headquarters of the local sailing club. In mediaeval times Arnside, like Preesall and Lytham, had salt pans and an 1895 survey refers to Saltcoat Farm near the church with mullion windows and carved door jambs, dated 1679. Ships called for this indispensable commodity up to the eighteenth century, when ore from Furness was shipped to Arnside. There was a fishery in 1760. High-grade peat was carted over Meathop Moss for farm use, coals imported from Whitehaven and marble and gunpowder was handled. Directories show the importance of Arnside's port trade, the sloop *Leighton* being built at Arnside especially for carrying iron and slate. Amongst master mariners, the landlord of the Fighting Cocks Inn, Captain Bush, once served as customs officer at this strong, stone-built customs warehouse. Underhill and Underwood, further down the road, were probably coastguards' cottages judging by their slit, look-out windows. Francis John Crossfield and descendants made the port esteemed for their boatbuilding, working at Church Street Yard and Beach Walk. Robert is the first mentioned in 1724 and other Crossfields built at Barrow. Into their 30ft Morecambe Bay prawners and yachts went local wood and workmanship akin to that of Armours and Singletons of Fleetwood.

With its grey stone Victorian and Edwardian villas, Arnside now seems more a place to retire to than sail from. Sea-going craft have become rarities, the deep gullies of the River Kent being havens for wading birds: avocet, black-headed gulls, turnstone, mallard and curlew. The upturned ship *Quartet*, part of a rusting anchor and massive iron cable chain found in the nettle-grown yard of Crossfields spoke eloquently of the port's past on our visits.

Above: The viaduct at Arnside, a train at the centre, *c.*1988. (Author's collection)

Left: Customs House, Arnside. (Author's collection)

Below: Crossfields boat builders – Arnside old port. (Author's collection)

The 1,300ft railway viaduct built across the River Kent, with its forty-six arches driven into 70ft of sand, represents a great Victorian engineering achievement by architect Brunlees, but it killed the shipping trade for Milnthorpe and other small ports. An early wooden jetty was replaced by a small pier built by Ulverston and Lancaster Railway Company. After the construction of the viaduct, because ships could no longer reach Milnthorpe the Railway Company granted compensation. A 1934 storm destroyed the end section and it was completely damaged by another fierce storm in 1983. Rebuilt by public subscription, there was a bunting-draped reopening in 1984.

Arnside had only twenty-three houses in the eighteenth century but when the railway arrived trade and population increased mightily. One directory reports the shore as 'covered one hour with ships, another with pedestrians' (1848). Henry VIII, a very port-conscious king, supplied an admiral, chosen from the powerful Clifford family, whose job it was to protect ships and the coast. The best anchorage was Bomershire Bay, lower down the river at Storth, a Norse word meaning 'woody place', where the landlord of the inn collected port dues; one of the oldest professions, smuggling, was probably indulged in, as a cellar behind the inn was uncovered in later years. It is a retreat similar to Wardleys and the Pilling Moss shore which was a veritable smugglers' corner in the eighteenth century but most of the marsh at Sandside, in the passage of time, has been carried away by the sea. Dixie's Inn used to have a ferry for which the ferryman charged threepence at high tide and sixpence at low. It was here in 1910 that six holiday makers from Oldham were drowned by the rapid tidal surge. Thomas North was one of many victims drowned crossing the sands in August 1924 although his horse and cart were saved by a sloop. Vessels were then calling at Sandside and Milnthorpe, bringing flour, sugar, rum, and salt. Twenty-five horses were needed for the unloading, which indicates brisk trade. Cargoes of sacking, twine, sailcloth, hemp and agricultural products were taken on board for the return journey.

The Furness Railway considerably influenced trade in these smaller ports as some goods previously carried by coastal vessels were transferred to the iron way. A link between the west coast main line at Hincaster Junction carried coke from County Durham to the Furness and West Cumberland ironworks. In 1942 passenger trains ceased at Sandside, freight continuing until 1968, but Sandside station disappeared, altering the landscape with the removal of Bela viaduct.

CHAPTER 24

GRANGE-OVER-SANDS

The town's name is derived from the grange or granary used by the Augustinian monks who lived at Cartmel Priory a mile away. The monks had a harbour for bringing in sea coal which they collected along the coast. It was a small but useful addition, helping in their tasks: fishing, oat growing and exporting wine for they had a vineyard also to tend. Wine went to the landing quay at Walney Island.

Grange-over-Sands Pier, 1900. (Author's collection)

CUMBRIA COUNTY COUNCIL
WARNING

The right of way across the bay to Hest Bank crosses dangerous sands. Do not attempt to cross without the official guide.

T. J. R. WHITFIELD
CLERK and CHIEF EXECUTIVE

GUIDE : MR. C. ROBINSON, GUIDES FARM, CART LANE, GRANGE - OVER - SANDS.

TELEPHONE : GRANGE - OVER - SANDS 2165 (EVENINGS ONLY)

Grange-over-Sands – a particularly dangerous area in Morecambe Bay with quicksands. (Author's collection)

Now a modern-day town, once reported as the Riviera of Cumbria, it is obvious why the monks chose this sheltered position and mild climate. Although the priory was relatively undamaged following the Dissolution of monasteries it has a door peppered with bullet holes – known as Cromwell's Door. The monks hid some precious items but must have been appalled to see Cromwell's troops stabling their horses amidst seventeenth-century carving in the church choir stalls.

Bathing is unwise because of treacherous tides in Morecambe Bay. Hampsfield Fell has a hospice which Thomas Remington, the vicar in the 1800s, built for travellers and from here there was a fine view of fells and sea-going vessels frantically being loaded during the hours between fast-flowing tides.

CHAPTER 25

MILNTHORPE AND GREENODD

Few signs remain of what was once the only port in Westmorland which sent vessels to Liverpool with slate, leather, casks of limestone and Sedgewick gunpowder. They returned with everyday articles to fill the pedlars' packs: clothes, ribbons and brushes. Ships unloaded opposite Dallam Tower on a bend in the River Bela (part of a stone wharf and an iron ring remain), sailing up at high water to land on gravelly shores. The goods were lowered into carts and as the tide ebbed, vessels settled on the hard bed, refloating on the next tide. Siltings led to moorings being made at Sandside and Arnside. Harbour dues went by rights to Levens Hall. The Kendal to Lancaster canal hastened the port's decline, but 'Milnthrop's heyday was between 1740 and 1850'. Small vessels carrying raw materials for the mills 'sailed up the Bela to unload at the Strands'. The Customs House is now the dairy in Park Road. Warehouses were in the village, near the scene of the photograph taken in the 1900s depicting the traditional fair. Edward I's Charter, confirmed in 1334, allowed a weekly market on Fridays and an annual fair in June. A flourishing corn market was established in 1810 and fifteen years later in May a remarkable statement was made:

> These fairs ... are held on Holy Thursday; the cattle which were brought in considerable numbers were almost literally devoured alive such was the eagerness of the buyers ... Such a fair as far as prices were concerned was never known in the memory of man. We understand 70 gentlemen sat down to a sumptuous dinner at the Cross Keys, Milnthrop.

Greenodd station in the peaceful days of May 1904 has passed into history. This spot is now a picnic area with a notice 'Beware of quicksands,' but following the estuary is a tell-tale, long, straight track, now grassed over, where once ran the railway. All that remains of Greenodd as a flourishing iron ore port are a few rotting staithes. Long before Fleetwood and Barrow, Greenodd and Penny Bridge were shipbuilding communities and it is interesting to learn both Greenodd and Ulverston were once creeks under the port of

Milnthorpe Fair.

Milnthorpe Fair, 1910. (Author's collection)

Lancaster. An early quay was built by Anthony Tissington and records prove the building of a brigantine, *Fortune,* in 1770 and its taking on of ore in 1780. A ship of over 300 tons was built at Penny Bridge although this small landing place and one at Spark Bridge were eventually rendered useless by silting. Timber, plentiful in the neighbourhood, and a good depth of water in a sheltered area were advantages in the port's favour. For making gunpowder at Low Wood factory sulphur and nitrates were brought. Imports of coal came from Whitehaven; coastwise from Coniston came copper and slate.

The iron steamer *Duke of Lancaster* was at Greenodd in 1866 and the port was yet another associated with the infamous slave trade. Liverpool's dreadful figures for slaves in 107 ships are 29,250; Lancaster's 950. Liverpool slavers left the black men at Penny Bridge to be collected by the agent from Storrs Hall, Windermere, whose owner was an acquaintance of William Wordsworth. Furness ports at one time exported 75,000 tons of iron ore per year. In the days of Lindale Moor Mining Company a miner was paid one shilling a day, a lad fourpence.

In the late eighteenth century and early nineteenth century, Greenodd, on the confluence of River Crake and River Leven, was a useful port, counted a creek of Lancaster. Iron ore, Cumberland slate, copper ore from Coniston Old Man mines, local limestone and gunpowder from Backbarrow were all exported from Greenodd. Imports were raw cotton and sugar. Ships were also built there.

The Ship Inn was originally a warehouse on the quay. When the Furness Railway line was built along the coast through Grange-over-Sands and Ulverston, track was laid to reach Greenodd, but most of that line has now gone, although a section is still being used by the Lakeside and Haverthwaite preserved Steam Railway. This connects with steamer sailings on Lake Windermere. When the slave trade was carried on Greenodd port was used by the tenant of Storrs Hall, now a hotel, as was Penny Bridge, a smaller calling place.

CHAPTER 26

ULVERSTON, BARDSEA AND CONISHEAD

Market Street, Ulverston. (Author's collection)

ULVERSTON

Traditionally, for three days in Whit week a hiring fair is held at the Gill, Ulverston. The scene in Market Street, 1920 photographed before the Martinmas Hiring Fair, between 11 November until 13 November, epitomised the once principal town, 'the emporium of Furness'. The *Kendal Mercury* on 24 August 1844 reported on visitors to Ulverston:

'This town has been full, never was there known by so many 'Lakers', on Wednesday last every inn was full to overflowing.' But it was also a busy port, although there is little sign of this is in the photograph. A canal was built 1¼ miles to the sea in 1795, opening into the River Leven channel and enclosing 1,000 acres of marshland. Ships of 400 tons, bringing coals, timber and merchandise, came to Ulverston, but alterations in the channel, 'impeded by banks of sand', troubled vessels.

Ainslie Pier, built by the North Lonsdale Iron & Steel Co. Ltd, was used to ship pig iron from Ulverston. Then the shortest, broadest and deepest canal in England, it is now used only by anglers. Records show that many strong ships were built to handle ore (2,000 tons a year of copper alone). Between 1830 and 1844 statistics add up to 36,000 tons. Rails for the building of Furness Railway were shipped here, although it was to take maritime trade. Examples of strong ships are *Coniston*, *Mary Goldsworthy*, *Eclipse*, *Bassa*, *Lord Oriel*, *Argo*, *Kate* and *Ulverston*. The removal of the Newland Company to Barrow and the drawing up of the Ramsden port plan ended the busy days of carpenters, captains, cordwainers, chandlers and shipbuilding on the canal banks. Richard and William Charnley, who were also captains, had built nine ships embodying a fine tradition of service, typical of north-west ports. William White, the last of the Ulverston ship builders, with his brother John, was noted for the expert workmanship which went into twelve wooden ships, including *Ellen Harrison*, *Millom Castle* and *Coniston*. As for the Furness Railway branch line, which originally carried passengers and freight, from Ulverston to Lakeside, the part remaining is the 3½-mile section from Haverthwaite connecting Windermere cruises, the pleasure boats plying the 10½-mile length of the lake.

The town gets its name from the Saxon 'Ulph'. After the Norman Conquest it became the property of the monks of Furness Abbey. Ulverston suffered from Scottish raiders under Robert the Bruce and again at the time of the Civil War but by the eighteenth century it had become a prosperous port and stopping place for Lancaster's Mail Coach. 'The London of Furness', however, began to silt up, the fate of so many seaports and towns seeking a link with the sea.

In 1795 the Ulverston Canal, 2 miles in length, helped trade to revive but it dwindled again and by 1940 was gone altogether. Fishermen and walkers enjoy the dock area now. Sir John Barrow, born in Ulverston in the eighteenth century, is commemorated by the monument on Hoad Hill. He was a Secretary to the Admiralty and a great geographer.

The Bardsea of August 1923 is seen as a limestone-walled village with two inns, the Ship and the Bradyll Arms. The former had a quay for ships from Morecambe Bay. Cockling and fishing were once rewarding employment – indeed a wayside sign one summer read: 'Cockles and fish for sale' – but wide stretches of bare, flat sand, wooded in parts down to the shore, gave slight indication of port days. The coast road to Barrow has atmosphere but few tangible signs of commercial shipping although I did see a carved, faded, blue, painted ship's figurehead of a mermaid. The

Angles and Vikings used this coast, making roads which lead to the thirteenth-century St Mary's Church at Urswick, whose stained-glass windows may have come from Furness Abbey. Next to Baycliff and Bardsea is Aldingham, its ancient church washed by high tides, an area which has lost more land over the centuries than any in the north-west. The church once stood in the centre of a parish which was reported in 1770 as having its greater part washed away. Low Scales village was once discernible at low tide but Crimleton and Rosse are known only in records as is the lost manor of Chornet at Rossall. Conishead's days as a port go back to monastic times when the Priory was founded by Gamel de Pennington who owned land in Ulverston and Bardsea. Industrious Conishead monks, like those of Furness, Cartmel and Cockersand, beside tilling the land, used the sea. (The monks of Cockersand set up a navigation light, cultivated coastal strips and worked salmon baulks.) Even after dissolution the rector of Cockersand still had the right of salmon catches at 'Parson's tides'. To a lesser extent so did Conishead, where the priory has long since vanished, replaced by a nineteenth-century gothic mansion which has suffered many changes, from Durham Miners' Convalescent Home to Manjushri Institute where Buddhists are in training. The changing scene offers house tours, exhibition and a craft shop, but further change is imminent with an application to convert Conishead Priory into four luxury dwellings. The 1780 Newland Iron Company which owned mines and furnaces built quays at Barrow, Greenodd and Conishead for the export of ores.

Conishead Priory, 1900. (Author's collection)

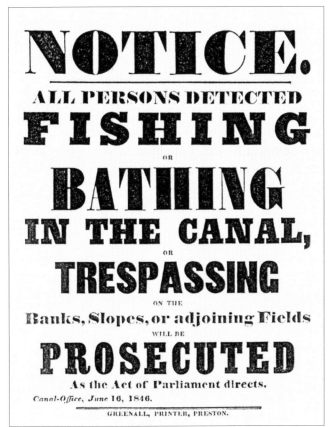

Ulverston Canal, nineteenth-century notice. (Author's collection)

Bardsea was an important port when iron ore mining was at its height but the railway and Ulverston Canal took the business of the port of Bardsea away so this once-busy industrial area of Furness is also given over to tourism.

On the edge of Morecambe Bay lies Bardsea Country Park and the well way-marked Conishead Priory, further enhanced by the Mahayana Buddhist Monks, who, on the occasions when the house is opened to the public, can point out the lake, grotto and hermitage amidst fine trees originally established by Gamel de Pennington.

CHAPTER 27

RAMPSIDE AND PIEL ISLAND

North-west fishermen, including members of the well-known Wright and Leadbetter families, used to attend courses at the fish hatchery sited on Piel Island, though these courses have long since passed into history. Piel is now a quiet yachting centre and base for the Barrow lifeboat, but there is a long shipping history attached to its name. Shipments of grain and wine were stored in Piel Castle by the Abbot of Furness in the 1200s, prior to being sent to Ireland. When Lambert Simnel landed at Piel from Dublin in 1487 with 2,000 German mercenaries the harbour was full of ships. It was once the most important in the district, its customs office the only customs point between Poulton-le-Sands and Whitehaven. The Barrow Harbour Act of 1848, when steamers were sailing regularly from Liverpool and Morecambe to Piel, also protected the harbour of Piel and its ancient rights. Storms partially wrecked Piel pier and John Abel Smith, entrepreneur involved in Fleetwood's building, sold out his rights on Roa Island to the Furness Railway Company. Further Railway and Harbour legislation gave the Company power to raise tolls on vessels using Piel Pier, such tolls to be not as substitution for but additional to tolls for use of the harbour. Until it became silted and eroded at the southern end when the channel altered course, this harbour was in use, though the pier was demolished in 1891.

PIEL ISLAND

Piel Island was used as a defence for Barrow Harbour. A castle was built there in the twelfth century but later the monks of Furness Abbey built a warehouse there for goods produced at the Abbey: wine, wool, honey and other foods. The ruins of their warehouse can still be seen. Piel Island can be reached by boat from Roa Island or by walking across the sands from Walney when it is safe to do so.

CHAPTER 28

BARROW-IN-FURNESS

—⁓⁓⁓—

Geographer H. Moll's map of 1724 includes 'Fourness Abbey, Aldingham, Ramside, Pile of Fouldrey, Walney,' but makes no mention of Barrow. It was in the eighteenth century a small village cashing in on the new craze of sea bathing, but also referred to as 'the first seaport in Furness for the exportation of iron ore, oats, malt and barley.' In forty years the Furness Railway transformed Barrow from a hamlet to a steel town of 60,000 people. The port was developed around the railway, which provided the means for bringing goods in from the area for export, and at its height encompassed 700 acres of water and busy quays.

Aiming for Liverpool standards, a custom house appeared in 1868. Speculators H.W. Schneider and James Ramsden quickly recognised its industrial potential. Further boost came from James Fisher & Sons, the most important shipowners, who inspired the building of blast furnaces, leading to what became known as the Haematite Steel company. Amongst Fishers' famous coastal steamers were *Mary Sinclair*, *Shoal Fisher* and *Lake Patos*. William Ashburner's was the first shipyard in 1867. Like the Iddons and the Cobbs, Captain Hugh Charnley and his four sons, all of whom became master mariners, were celebrated seafarers, their fame spreading down the coast and to ports across the world. Thomas sailed out of Fleetwood and the first Trinity House pilot at Barrow was a Charnley. To the 33-acre Buccleuch Dock and 30-acre Devonshire Dock were added Ramsden Dock Basin and Cavendish Dock. All berths on the south side of the first two are now owned by Vickers Shipbuilding and Engineering Ltd, used exclusively for shipbuilding. Dreadnoughts were built in Devonshire Dock about 1910. Vickers' order book was worth £1 billion; a £1 million contract having been announced on 8 September 1987. The firm pre-dates that by ninety years and Barrow Docks have supplied ships for the Royal Navy since 1852, as well as submarines from the first one to present-day nuclear types. On Trafalgar Day 1960, HM the Queen launched *Dreadnought*, sixteen months after the laying of its keel.

Above: Launch of Vickers' Naval Airship at Barrow. (Author's collection)

Left: Princess Margaret's visit to the docks, 1952. (Author's collection)

Barrow Town Hall could be seen on clear days from Fleetwood. Local pensioners, known as the 'Fleetwood Parliament', would vie to tell the time from the massive clock tower. (Author's collection)

HMS *Invincible*, another famous name, was launched in March 1980. The original Barrow Shipbuilding Company became Naval Construction and Armament, then Vickers Sons and Maxim Ltd, later Vickers Armstrong Ltd, and eventually Vickers Shipbuilding and Engineering Ltd. Shown above is one of many launches from Vickers Naval Construction Works, that of a naval airship. To the same place came HRH Princess Margaret, the Queen's sister, in 1952. Amongst the officials on the quay was Lord Derby, Lord Lieutenant of Lancashire. Test pilot Neville Duke in a Hawker Hunter led an air display in her honour, while she also had a trip across Morecambe Bay in HMS *Coquette*, and enjoyed a meal of Finnan haddock topped with a poached egg.

At this important port a covered modern construction hall with ship lift has been provided at Devonshire Dock to preserve secrets from satellite photography, especially the £425 million Trident scheme so important to the nation. James Fisher and Sons provide stevedoring services. Fishers, the sole Lloyd's agent at the port, have a floating crane of 200 tons capacity. In addition to British Nuclear Fuel and British Gas traffic, Tilcon Ltd export locally produced limestone from Anchor Lime Basin. With 220 acres of land and over 350 acres of water the Associated British port of Barrow is the biggest dock system between Mersey and Clyde.

A most difficult job was the lowering of the lock sill at Devonshire Dock many years ago to allow larger vessels to pass, always a highly skilled operation because explosives could not be used.

The Barrow Harbour Act of 1848 sanctioned the appointment of the Barrow Harbour Commission, laid down the boundaries of Barrow Harbour and provided against injury to Piel Harbour. In 1852, Piel Pier was partially wrecked by a severe storm and John Abel Smith sold out his property and rights at Roa Island to the Furness Railway Company (Furness Railway Act of 1853).

The Furness Railway Act and Barrow Harbour Act of 1855 gave the Furness Railway powers to raise tolls on vessels using the Piel Pier, but laid down that these tolls:

> Shall not be in substitution or satisfaction for any tolls or dues which are or may be legally recoverable from or in respect of vessels using the Harbour of Piel, but shall be demanded and recovered in addition to any such tolls or dues.

Postcard showing some of the sights of Barrow. (Author's collection)

On board the
Lady Muyra
off Barrow
(pleasure steamer,
1912). (Author's
collection)

In the 1990s Barrow fitted out the helicopter carrier HMS *Ocean* and constructed the
Wave class tankers *Wave Knight* and the amphibious assault ships HMS *Bulwark* and
HMS *Albion*. Barrow is also a gas terminal and other exports are woodpulp, limestone
to Scandinavia, and also the handling of shipments of nuclear fuels and radioactive
waste for BNFL's Sellafield plant.

When gas was discovered in Morecambe Bay in 1985 the Rampside area, south
of Barrow, handled its processing. The wind farm off Walney Island, something of a
surrealistic scene viewed from the shore, sends the electricity generated to Heysham
via an undersea cable.

The interesting Dock Museum has arisen on what was the old graving dock and
the port, owned by Associated British Ports Holdings, is at present considered a minor
port. However there are plans afoot to create a cruise ship terminal at Barrow and the
powerful firm of James Fisher and Sons founded in 1847 continues to cover all aspects
of marine engineering. One wonders what would the monks of Furness Abbey, once
the second richest Cistercian abbey in Britain, have thought?

PS *PRINCE OF WALES II* 1886

Built by the Barrow Ship Building Company in 1886 for the Fleetwood service, the
Prince of Wales II was the last paddle steamer used by the Lancashire and Yorkshire
Railway Company on the Royal Mail route between Fleetwood and Belfast. She was
the largest paddle steamer in the fleet with a gross tonnage of 1,429. The paddle steamer
was eventually sold in 1896.

CHAPTER 29

WALNEY ISLAND AND BIGGAR BANK

—◦◦◦—

In 1908 a bridge was built to make the connection for the ferry route between Barrow and Walney Island, replacing the steam ferry. Hundreds of years before this the monks of Furness smelted iron ore on Walney in bloomeries and had a fleet of ships. A lighthouse was erected on the southern tip of Walney in 1799 to assist the North Head Lighthouse at St Bee's Head and the Morecambe Bay Light vessel whose shortcoming was that in stormy conditions it could break free and mislead shipping. On 23 January 1836 a tremendous gale struck, driving *Angelique* onto the Isle of Walney where she was lost with all hands.

Walney, the largest of the Furness islands, protects Barrow harbour. Smaller islands are Roa, Sheep and Piel, the latter known as Pile of Fouldry. In 1423 the Abbot of Furness was accused of smuggling wool out of the county from 'Peele de Foddray'. Flocks of seabirds frequent the houses on Roa Island where once the pilots lived who brought boats up Walney channel. Rampside has a deep natural basin, the Conckhole, which gives its name to the Conckle Inn and is reminiscent of Canshe Hole, another deep natural basin in the River Wyre, used for safe anchorage long before a port was built. Many times the tide has crossed the whole island of Walney. Biggar Dyke was one of many made by the monks of Furness to prevent this. Sand and gravel were unloaded here at a small pier. Tradition has it that a Spanish galleon from the Armada fleet was wrecked, its beams and other timbers going into the making of the inn, the Queen's Head.

Promenade, Walney Island. (Author's collection)

The Swings, Biggar Bank, Walney Island. (Author's collection)

CHAPTER 30

MILLOM AND RAVENGLASS

—◦◦◦—

MILLOM

On the western side of the Duddon estuary Millom grew around its castle built in the fourteenth century. It was the mining influence that made this little town prosperous. By the nineteenth century there were eleven working shafts and in 1968 the last of the workings closed; however, by then the town had grown considerably. At Haverigg was the old Hodbarrow Iron Mount, a replica of this, and a miner's cottage being interesting sights at the Folk Museum.

Millom had cheap shipping facilities attractive to Barrow and Ulverston, so many beautiful schooners were built here. Thomas and William Postlethwaite's shipyard was very successful. The small yard of William Anderson & Sons was noted for fine quality workmanship in yachts and fishing boats such as *Ixia*, built in 1913. The whole area was honeycombed with iron workings, but Hodbarrow was conveniently adjacent to Millom wharf. A reconstruction of these mines and of miners' cottages can be viewed at Millom Folk Museum. The coaster *Duke*, built 1927, called regularly at Millom to load up with pig iron. Fleetwood fishermen and Cornish miners came to Millom to use their skills. A Welsh and Irish connection was established by the trading of iron ore to South Wales and on to Ireland with coal. One of the Welshmen, William Morgan, became harbour master. The Hodbarrow Mining Company had shares in the schooners which sailed as far as South America, representing also the Duddon Shipping Association. *Nellie Bywater*, a two-masted schooner, was 'A1 at Lloyd's' for twelve years. The tug *Borwick Rails*, built 1888 and sold to Whitehaven, was not scrapped until the 1970s. Tugs *Duddon* and *Hardback*, the latter used at Millom for twenty years, proved equally strong and powerful. All down the coast, quality boat building coupled with superb seamanship is seen to have been a hallmark of the nineteenth century and beyond. It was necessary to provide buoys, lighthouse and pier in the tricky Duddon channel

Above: Scenes of Ravenglass, Cumbria, possibly used by the Romans as a calling-place. A fort existed, linking it with Hardknott. (Author's collection)

Below: Ravenglass, 1975. (Author's collection)

for the safety of brigs, flats, schooners and sloops. Fittingly, *Harriet* FDIII was piloted through Duddon's shifting shoals in 1977 by Alec Mellor, B.E.M. pilot at Haverigg. A trawler skipper who had sailed the Irish Sea for fifty years, he saw the ironworks close and the departure of the boats which once carried pig iron. The famous 60ft Fleetwood trawler built in 1893 by Singletons and still the holder of the Fleetwood record for hake was bought by sculptress Josephina Banner, founder of Action Now, as a centre for young disabled people. After *Harriet*'s safe arrival at Borwick Rails Alec Mellor supervised the removal of the engine, restored the hull and set about re-rigging her for her new role.

During the second century the Romans built forts at Ambleside, Ravenglass and Hardknott, part of a chain of coastal defences linked to Hadrian's Wall. Outlet and landing from the sea would probably favour Ravenglass. The forts Brocavum and Galava, the latter at Ambleside, were kept busy when the war-like tribe of the Brigantes rose against Roman occupation. Galava, of which vestigial remnants can still be seen, (although nothing compared with Hardknott) would have consisted of timber buildings and turf ramparts. As at Ribchester in Lancashire there appears to have been a civilian population within the ramparts.

Some of these forts were later built of stone and although few signs of a Roman presence remain at Galava (sunken grassy areas along the shores of Windermere Lake) this fort once housed 500 soldiers but by AD400 the troops that had fought the Lakeland Brigantes were sent back to Rome and the forts dismantled. Brovacum fort lasted longer but part of its stone was later built into the entrance of Brougham Castle. At Ravenglass, three rivers meet; the Esk, the Mite and the Irk. The Romans built a fort here called Glannaventa and the Bath House still remains in a good state of preservation. There is good anchorage from the sea and fishing is a thriving industry.

Ravenglass is the terminus of the Ravenglass and Eskdale Railway, a narrow-gauge railway which runs for 7 miles through picturesque countryside. 'L'aal (little) Ratty' as it is affectionately called, was built in 1875 to carry iron ore to the Furness Railway.

A postcard of Ravenglass, showing Munster Castle and 'L'aal Ratty', the miniature steam engine, pulling in the tourists. (Author's collection)

This picture is taken from a pier. The boats are fishing boats, except the middle one which is a Pilot boat. (Author's collection)

CHAPTER 31

WHITEHAVEN

—◦◦◦—

In the 1600s Whitehaven was a small fishing hamlet but the Lowther family set about exploiting the coalfields on land which they owned and for this they needed a better harbour which was built in the seventeenth century. Mining shafts explored deep beneath the sea. Tobacco was imported from America. Old quays and harbour works can still be seen and Whitehaven Museum has artefacts from early seafaring days. The enormous sandstone cliff of St Bees Head, 300ft high, with its lighthouse offers wonderful views of the Isle of Man.

In the early 1700s the town was one of the major ports in Britain, its prosperity founded on the coal and iron trade. The harbour at Whitehaven still handles cargo and its deepest pit, Haig colliery, Cumbria's last deep coal mine, closed in 1986, ending 700 years of mining history in the area. There is now a museum at the site of the former colliery.

Coal mining dates back to the thirteenth century when the monks from St Bees Abbey supervised the opening of coal mines at Arrowthwaite. John Paul Jones who captained the pirate ship *Ranger* learned much about the port because he had trained there as an apprentice ship's hand. He attempted in 1778 to attack Whitehaven but his venture failed. That episode was during the American War of Independence when James was an American naval commander. Whitehaven once had only six fishermen's cottages and a single sea-going vessel, the *Bee*.

Whitehaven docks in 1897 was at that time the chief port of Cumberland and the principal town of a busy colliery district. Situated on a creek about 3 miles north of the Head of St Bee's, the harbour and wet dock area, protected by two stone piers, west and north, each extend almost 1,000ft out to sea, with several quays between. Victorian times saw these very busy with the export of coal and iron and a large import trade in timber and grain. Regular packet steamers plied to Silloth, Isle of Man, Liverpool, Dublin, Belfast and Dundrum. One of the region's oldest ports, it was counted the

Marchon Enterprise on its maiden voyage from Whitehaven Port in 1962, owned by the firm Albright and Wilson. (Author's collection)

third in Great Britain in the eighteenth century because of large quantities of tobacco and sugar imports. Coal and iron exporting made it noteworthy, a coal trade with Ireland going back to 1680.

By the eighteenth century 250 vessels were employed in this trade. Big demand was made on local shipbuilders T. and J. Brocklebank, Robert Hardy, William Wilson and William Bowes. The oldest shipping line in the country was founded by Daniel Brocklebank of Whitehaven, which was taken over by Whitehaven Shipbuilding Company, builders of *Candida*, *Patterdale* and the 1,700-ton *Thirlmere*, launched in 1874. High standards, as with the Lune Shipbuilding Co., led to liquidation, but an iron ship of 1,355 tons, *Dunboyne*, was launched in 1888 after the firm had reopened in 1880. Whitehaven ships were noted for their strong appearance. Vessels like *Burdwan*, *Bowfell* and *Cambray* went to Virginia with gunpowder and general goods, the last they saw of home being the North Pier lighthouse built in 1841. In the nineteenth century an average of 4,500 vessels sailed to and from Whitehaven every year. A small fleet of fishing boats continues that tradition, the photograph of West Strand fish market, 4 September 1904, recalling those days, when on the sides of Cumberland Omnibuses the Laundry slogan ran, 'We return everything but the dirt.'

Left: North Pier Lighthouse, Whitehaven, built 1841. (Author's collection)

Below: The Docks, Whitehaven, 1890. (Author's collection)

The ship *Marchon Enterprise* was tailor-made for the Queen's Dock. Sister ship *Marchon Venturer*, built at Wallsend, made 275 trips to Casablanca for cargoes of phosphate rock. They lie off Whitehaven whilst cargoes are ferried into dock by *Marchon Enterprise* and *Odin*, a motorised barge. The *Marchon Venturer* still operates under general charter, carrying cargoes of coal and scrap steel, flying the flag of Annan Shipping Company, whilst her skipper and eleven-man crew have rejoined James Fisher & Co.'s pool of seamen at Barrow. Fishers have managed the ship for Albright and Wilson Ltd since she was launched in 1962. The life-saving apparatus station at Whitehaven in 1909 represents a round the coast feature. The Board of Trade awarded a shield annually to the life-saving apparatus company in Great Britain and Northern Ireland which performed the best wreck service. In 1932 it was won by *Craighouse Jura* for the outstanding rescue operation of eleven men from the steam trawler *Craik*, wrecked off the Sound of Islay

Left: Life-saving apparatus station, Whitehaven, 1900s. (Author's collection)

Below: West Strand fish market, Whitehaven, 4 September 1904. (Author's collection)

CHAPTER 32

WORKINGTON AND MARYPORT

WORKINGTON

The sources of wealth for Workington situated on the River Derwent were iron and coal. Ships from all over the world once called at this deep-water port and it was yet another involved in the slave trade. One revealing letter reads: 'The struggle for slaves was so great that Captain Watts of Pool gave £15 per head, Captain Dodson of Lancaster from the Marquis of Granby £14 which is very dear.' In 1767 six years after the letter was written, the *Marquis of Granby*, 90 tons burthen, was lost off Workington, outward bound for Sierra Leone, carrying mixed cargo. The photograph from 1913 of Moss Bay, Workington, shows

A factory chimney falls, 1913, Workington. (Author's collection)

Maryport, 1903. (Author's collection)

another disaster, the collapse of a huge factory chimney, Williamson & Son. In the early 1800s 170 ships were registered. These shipped coal from nearby collieries to southern England. Workington was still used to handle railway lines until 2006, when the last local steelworks closed down. From 1890 onwards R. Williamson & Son produced a fleet of coasters and in 1900 the impressive *Horn* for Germany. Workington's Lonsdale dock which opened in 1865 could not accommodate deep-sea steamers, but in 1927 the Prince of Wales dock was opened. Workington's shipping history is well displayed in the Helena Thompson Museum.

Sandy beaches lie between the ports of Cumbria and Lancashire. The Romans built fort Alauna to forestall any storming of Hadrian's Wall. The name 'Mary' is associated with the wife of Humphrey Senhouse who, in the eighteenth century, built docks and a harbour. The coastal coalfields drew the attention of developers and produced a number of ports along this Cumbria stretch. Iron rails were sent all over the world when railways were promoted. Humphrey named the Elizabeth Dock after a daughter. Business declined over the years as the harbour silted up. There are now empty berths on North Quay, Maryport and an almost deserted harbour where ships from all over the world once unloaded cargo.

Humphrey in 1756 changed its place name, Ellenfoot (Alnefoot), naming it after his wife Mary, by developing the creek at the mouth of the River Ellen. Previously ships were registered at Whitehaven, but with Customs House and Harbour Office it became a port in its own right. Shipbuilders were Jonathon Middleton, Robert Ritson & Company and K. Wood & Sons. Until the First World War boats were launched broadside on because of the narrow river mouth and subsequent shallow water, as was the case with *Lycidas* from Ritsons. This practice was followed in some cases at

Fleetwood. Commander Henry Mangles Denham, hydrographer, who surveyed the Mersey, Dee and Wyre, suggested improvements for Maryport and other Cumberland ports. A list of Cumberland shipping, 1840, shows 113 vessels registered at Maryport and by the 1880s the Holme Line had over twenty vessels travelling to the St Lawrence River and Montreal, taking rails and bringing back corn and timber. They also travelled to Hobart, Tasmania, carrying wool on the return trip. Well-known captains included Tweedie, Johnson, Brown and Gorley, the last three working with the Holme Line. Records also refer to fishing. The *Zephyretta*, a herring boat from Poulton-le-Sands (the early name for Morecambe), was returning manned by Robert Baxter, Richard Lupton and Richard Gardner when a gale struck and sank her on Clark's wharf. The port which was once very busy is now merely a refuge for shipping, but vigorous attempts are afoot to revitalise Maryport, even if it means bringing in new light industries. The docks are closed to commercial traffic and plans are under way for a marina, using the nostalgic old harbour, docks area and quayside. It is a port full of history, well displayed in its Maritime Museum. In 1716 Humphrey and Eleanor Senhouse lived at Bank House Farm; half a mile away at Ewanrigg Hall lived the Christian family who worked mines and shipped coal in the eighteenth century. One sea-faring member, Fletcher Christian, is associated with the notorious mutiny on the *Bounty*. Tiles and slates from a Roman fort came to light when the hillsides of Sea Brows were being quarried for the stone that went into Senhouse Dock, but all the workings are now overgrown with brambles and gorse. Oystercatchers, dunlins, wild geese, grey seals and porpoises plunge and swim off Maryport pier.

The Naval Reserve Station at Maryport, photographed on 23 September 1903, and cobbled Fleming Square, one of the largest in the north-west with its once noisy butter market, are well remembered with a fund of anecdotes from older residents. The River Ellen, once famous for its salmon, now attracts anglers hunting trout; such are the shifting, fluctuating fortunes of a seaport, but new industries and high technology promise to bring back Maryport's fame, which is what the younger generation are interested in.

EGREMONT

A tiny town of colour-washed houses, it has a ruined, Norman castle dating from 1130 but only part of the outer walls are left. The River Eben has charm but Egremont is remembered for its annual Crab Fair. No, not the mollusc, but small crab apples. It is a fair that goes back to the seventeenth century when the fruits were given to visitors. Egremont's Apple Cart is a novelty, paraded at the time of the Fair along with a stand-in model for William de Meschines in mediaeval dress. He built the castle.

CHAPTER 33

SILLOTH

———✦✦✦———

This Associated British Port linked with Barrow has considerable room for modern expansion and is currently striving to realise its potential. The main feature of New Dock at Silloth is the production plant of Carr's Flour Mill on the north side. On the south is extensive modern lairage, covered accommodation for 800 head of cattle, cement storage silos, at the east end, D.A. Harrison's warehouse. Imports of bulk grain and live cattle have been the port's principal traffic for years, but bulk cement, animal foodstuffs and dried milk now make up the major part of cargo handling. Fertilisers, wood pulp and molasses also feature and the suction elevator which can shift 150 tons per hour has storage capacity for 7,000 tons.

1933 port statistics for Silloth, when steam coasters from the Liverpool firm of J.S. Monks called, show the following commodities: basic slag, coal, grain, fish, slates, timber, pyrites, phosphates, coke, flour, gypsum, copper cinders; imports 62,815 tons, exports 33,980 tons.

The railway made Silloth into a holiday resort, although bathing at low tide is dangerous because of strong tidal currents, the sea ebbing for one mile and perilous on the flood. The construction of Marshall Dock, the tidal outer basin, was signalled by the 1855 Silloth and Silloth Bay Railway and Dock Act. In 1869 there existed a mile-long railway viaduct across the Firth of Forth to the Scottish shore, providing a direct link between the iron ore mines of Cumberland and the smelting furnaces or Lanarkshire. Coupled with shipping, Silloth was, for a time, a small but bustling port. However, in 1875 the bridge pillars of the viaduct froze and cracked, ice-floes doing more damage. It was repaired and trains ran until 1920 but such was the expense in 1935 that the viaduct was demolished. Because of silting at Port Carlisle, Silloth had become useful for Liverpool, Douglas and Dublin sailings operated by the Silloth Bay Steam Navigation Company Ltd.

The monks from Furness Abbey encouraged farming on the Solway marshes and a long-standing salt industry was established by Cistercian monks, but today's Silloth is more inclined to the tourist industry: to boats moored in a marina rather than ships in a dock.

Furness Abbey, built in the twelfth century on a peninsula between Morecambe Bay and Duddon river mouth. Chapter House and the refectory remain. (Author's collection)

The Green, Silloth. This general view of Silloth town dates from 1929. (Author's collection)

The nineteenth century saw Silloth busy as a harbour for coastal shipping but the coming of the railway in 1856 made it popular as a holiday resort. This part of Cumbria has treacherous sands but views out to the Solway Firth brought in keen walkers further attracted by a lack of commercialism.

Long before the idea of pleasure and leisure in an attractive resort, the Cistercian monks from Holme Cultram Abbey grew grain and like the Furness Abbey monks established a useful salt industry. Their granaries were called laths so 'sea laths' led to the name Silloth.

Although the harbour is small, ships still bring in grain for a local large flour mill. All the holiday attractions can be found around The Green, shown on the previous page.

Port Carlisle, established 1819, to provide a harbour for shipping following the coast, and linked by canal to the city of Carlisle, suffered major changes in the 1860s by shifts in tidal currents. The harbour silted up and it is now hard to find any traces of it. When the long-awaited Grand Survey of the British Isles appeared it made clear the magnitude of natural forces, waves and tidal streams continually bringing about physical changes especially affecting river estuaries. Between 1848 and 1854 accurate sets of maritime charts appeared. Principal ports established harbour boards with the aim of regular maritime surveying. Fearon and Eyes, Murdoch Mackenzie and P.P. Burdett had made hydrographic surveys, the findings of the last mentioned on Formby Channel, adding much to the seafarer's safety. Lieutenant H.M. Denham did valuable work in Liverpool Bay and along the west coast. The creation of the Mersey Docks and Harbour Board in 1857 led to a close watch on channels and banks.

Amongst service vessels essential to any port, operating off the north-west coast were sand suction dredgers, hopper barges, grab hoppers, tenders, coal barges, sandpumps, pilot schooners and bucket dredgers with such names as *Fylde, Neptune, Blackpool, Lytham, Wyvern, Guide, Conqueror* and *Furness*. Without these 'old groaners' and workhorses, ports would have come to a standstill.

CHAPTER 34

HAVERIGG AND SEATHWAITE

─◦◦◦─

HAVERIGG

From the estuary of the River Esk at Ravenglass to that of the River Duddon there lies a 12-mile stretch of shingle, sea wrack, marram grass and blowing sands. Haverigg, a small village, has been left a legacy of disused ironstone mines on one side and a picturesque backdrop of sand dunes. Spent quarries have been flooded to form Hodbarrow Hollow Lake, part of a Country Park, the haunt of sea birds. On a clear day one can see for miles. There are fine views across to Walney Island and Barrow. A sense of isolation takes hold.

Haverigg seems to express the right note to end a review of calling places, harbours and ports of the north-west coast: a calm acceptance of the past being overtaken by the future. As in so many of these once small ports industry has been exchanged for a form of tourism which shows an honest attempt to enshrine the past. I wonder what that indefatigable curate, the Revd Robert Walker of Seathwaite, not so far away, would have thought of such a change. Would he have put together a smaller version of Blackpool's 'Big One' from scrap iron? A craft shop perhaps? I feel sure he would have had some good ideas.

SEATHWAITE

The Seathwaite clipping stone was used by Revd Walker as a stool for shearing sheep. He was an eighteenth-century curate who, it was said, rose at 4a.m. in summer and 5a.m. in winter. When he married he was earning £5 a year but managed to raise a family of eight augmenting his income by spinning, weaving, shearing, brewing, doctoring and teaching. Aged ninety-three when he died, he left £2,000 to his family. Robert's fame spread beyond Seathwaite and the Duddon Valley. The then-Poet Laureate William Wordsworth mentions Robert in his series of sonnets, 'The River Duddon'.

Other titles published by The History Press

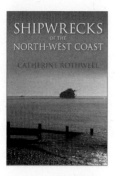

Shipwrecks of the North-West Coast
CATHERINE ROTHWELL

The north-west coast of England is renowned for its fierce storms, with the inevitable loss of life, damage, shipwrecks, attending lifeboats and emerging heroism aroused by such perilous situations. Catherine Rothwell has spent forty-nine years on the Fylde coast, fascinated with the sea in all its moods. Illustrated with images of ships, wrecks, mariners and ports, this book is a unique guide to the shipwrecks of the north-west.

978-0-7524-5307-1

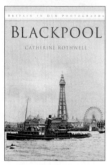

Blackpool in Old Photographs
CATHERINE ROTHWELL

Blackpool, that fine example of Victorian enterprise, made the most of its 7 miles of flat, golden sands and, with the help of the railways, workers were speedily brought in and captivated by its splendid buildings and fairytale interiors. The crowds came in their thousands year after year for seaside holidays to 'wonderful Blackpool, the most progressive resort under the flag'. This book is a fabulous record of the growth of Blackpool into the national treasure it is today.

978-0-7524-4950-0

Liverpool in Old Photographs
CATHERINE ROTHWELL

This book brings to life the famous port, historic streets and outstanding architecture of Liverpool, a 'city of change and challenge'. Through over 200 photographs and a healthy dose of grit and humour, many fine tales are told of those who flocked to the city in the nineteenth century, hoping for a new life in the New World, as well as of Liverpool's continuing phoenix-like quality of survival.

978-0-7524-4941-8

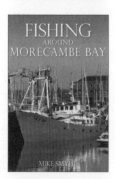

Fishing Around Morecambe Bay
MIKE SMYLIE

Maritime historian Mike Smylie takes the reader on a journey through the history of fishing in Morecambe Bay, featuring Barrow, Ulverston, Grange-over-Sands, Morecambe, Glasson and Fleetwood. Using over 170 local photographs, the book covers a variety of topics, from salmon fishing and cockle-picking to fishing on horseback, ensuring it will appeal to fishing enthusiasts and those interested in the area's coastal history alike.

978-0-7524-5393-4

Visit our website and discover thousands of other History Press books.

www.thehistorypress.co.uk